Your
30-Day
Retirement Plan

*Simple strategies to transform your olden
years into your golden years*

The 30-Day Retirement Plan

Patrick T. Lyman, CAS, CSA, RFC, RHU

To my wife: B, without your steady hand keeping me focused and grounded and your unconditional love, support, and encouragement over the years, I would never have had the courage to tackle, and more importantly, finish this book. This one's for you.

I would also like to thank my three terrific kids—Kristen, Colin, and Geoff. You have inspired me to be the best I can be, always.

The 30-Day Retirement Plan

PRAISE FOR *YOUR 30-DAY RETIREMENT PLAN*

"*Your 30-Day Retirement Plan* is a great book! I am already recommending to people because it covers more than your traditional retirement book written today. It has a very holistic feel and is a very easy book to understand and follow."

-- Steven Tepfenhart
Senior Business Development Specialist

"*Your 30-Day Retirement Plan* is an excellent overview of the multitude of issues one needs to consider during the retirement planning process. It doesn't overload the reader, who may be a novice to retirement planning, with too many details from the get go. For someone actively engaged in planning, this book may remind them of issues they have overlooked."

--Cynthia Sabatini

"*Your 30-Day Retirement Plan* was a great read and written to make a substantially heavy subject much easier to digest. It got me thinking about my own financial planning needs as well as those of my younger relatives just finishing up college and getting their first real jobs. I liked the daily breakdown—doing one task a day, whatever it may be, definitely makes things seem much more manageable. This book simplified a complicated topic, but not overly so."

-- Kelly R. Koscil, Esquire

Table of Contents

Patrick T. Lyman, CAS, CSA, RFC, RHU

Introduction

A Plan for You

Retirement planning is one of the most important tasks we need to complete to plan for our future. Yet, too many of us aren't actually doing it. Don't take my word for it; look at the facts:

- In 2016 *Time* magazine reported that 33 percent of Americans had saved nothing for retirement.
- According to *Time* magazine, as of 2016 only 13 percent of baby boomers had saved $300,000 or more for retirement.[1]
- CNBC reported in 2016 that 40 percent of millennials had no retirement planning strategy in place.

---

[1]http://time.com/money/4258451/retirement-savings-survey/

- Marketwatch reported in 2015 that 37 percent of generation X workers had done nothing—*nothing*—to plan for their finances during retirement.

Frankly, if these numbers don't spell crisis, then I don't know what does. There is a truly interesting trend that comes through these numbers, and that's one of the things that drove me to write this book. Perhaps you noticed it too: every generation, from millennials to boomers, is struggling with retirement planning.

This isn't just a boomer problem, which you might expect it to be since they are the closest to retirement age. It's a problem for middle-aged gen Xers who often feel like they don't have enough information to start planning. It's also a problem for millennials, who've been scarred by low employment rates, the Great Recession of 2007 to 2009, and crippling student loan debt.

Sadly, this is a problem that unites us. It's a problem for high-earners and low-earners, young and old. And the more we ignore this problem, the bigger a burden it's going to be for the entire country. Already, 45 percent of retirees are relying on Social Security for their main source of income.[2] And the average monthly benefit? It's just $1,503.[3] So 45 percent of retirees are relying on a mere $1,503 to get them through their monthly expenses. As more and more boomers retire, the number of retirees relying on Social Security will climb. Yet in the workforce, the number of

---

[2] https://www.ssa.gov/news/press/factsheets/basicfact-alt.pdf

[3] https://www.aarp.org/retirement/social-security/questions-answers/maximum-ss-benefit/

workers paying Social Security taxes is *declining*, which means that Social Security tax rates will likely rise, giving millennials, younger baby boomers, and gen Xers even less income to set aside for their own retirement.

I want to be honest and disclose that I am telling you these facts to scare you. Why? Because you need to be scared. Make no mistake about it, I'm scared as well. I'm scared about the future this is going to create for my children and grandchildren. I'm scared for all the boomers and gen Xers who are setting themselves up for a financially insecure and uncomfortable retirement—if they can even take one at all. And I'm scared for the millennials who are barely starting their careers, already saddled with debt and a frequent sense of hopelessness about their financial future.

But there's a reason I want you to be scared. I want your fear to motivate you into changing this situation. I want your fear to push you into doing something differently. Frankly, I want this to make you start planning.

To do that, we have to stop running away when we hear the term, "retirement planning." It sounds vague and overwhelming, but it doesn't have to be. In fact, as I'm going to show you in this book, you can create a solid retirement plan by doing just one small activity a day for thirty days. You read that right: one activity a day for thirty days is all it takes to help create a secure retirement plan that offers you safety and comfort during your golden years.

Why Thirty Days?

As a financial advisor, I spend the majority of my workday speaking with people about their financial plans. The people who come to my office are generally ready to get started. They're ready to receive help and guidance, and they're prepared to start making changes according to the plan we put in place.

But I also talk to a lot of people from day to day who aren't seeking a financial advisor. From the person I make small talk with in the elevator, to my doctor, to the people I socialize with. When I talk to them and they learn about my profession, the topic often moves to retirement planning. While their questions for me sometimes seem like cries for help, I also sense that they are so overwhelmed by the idea of retirement planning that they shut down and simply try to ignore the problem for another day.

I'm not the kind of person who oversteps my boundaries. I know that money and financial planning are intensely personal and private endeavors. But it's extremely frustrating to know that I could help every single one of these people secure a stable retirement, if they would only ask.

That's why I developed the 30-Day Retirement Plan. With this program, I've boiled down retirement planning into thirty relatively simple tasks that everyone can do on a lunch break at work, after putting the kids to bed, or in the morning before heading off to work. With this book, I've essentially given you a roadmap to a secure financial future, and all you have to do is follow the trail I've marked.

How This Book Is Designed

When I developed this book, I wanted to make sure that you, the reader, felt like you had ultimate control. I also wanted to make sure you had enough information because, after all, how can you be in control if you don't really understand what you're doing? Isn't every destination easier to get to when you have a roadmap?

I've laid out this book so that every chapter is dedicated to a single day's task. I think this makes the idea of retirement planning much less overwhelming and it makes you more likely to keep moving forward with your own plan. You can decide to do these tasks one-a-day in the order they appear, or you can skip around and do the easier ones on days you're extra busy. If you want, you can even group a few days' activities together and accomplish them in one go. It's not important how you do these tasks, it's simply important that you do them.

At the end of each chapter, I've included a checklist:

Day 1 Checklist

☐ Think about which kind of IRA is going to be best for your retirement objectives.

In addition to the daily checklist, you'll also find generation-specific tips throughout the book. The generations I focused on are:

	Millennials Born between 1981 and 1997

	Gen X Born between 1965 and 1980

	Baby Boomers Born between 1946 and 1964

There's a reason that I wanted to give added tips based on generation. Each generation is dealing with its own unique set of financial challenges and concerns regarding retirement planning. While boomers are headed for retirement now or in the next few years and are concerned about how to make distributions last while minimizing tax responsibilities, millennials are concerned about the best way to grow their savings so they can retire on their own terms—all while dealing with crushing student loans and a shaky political and employment environment. Gen Xers, often at the peak of their careers, are dealing with the fact that they didn't save aggressively enough in the past, so now they need to make up for that all while considering how they might help their children deal with college costs.

With the generation-specific tips sprinkled throughout this book, you'll hopefully find solutions that are specific to the concerns your generation is facing, while also getting a glimpse of the strategies you may need to employ later as you age.

Make This Book Your Own

My goal with this book is to help you create a financially secure future. I'm going to cover all kinds of topics—from helping you create a bucket list to developing a savings plan, from thinking about your legacy plan and your health to paying off your debt. Over the next thirty days, we're going to leave no stone unturned, and we're going to do that in a way that's not overwhelming. When you're done reading this book and implementing these action steps, you're going to feel better than you ever have about your future, and you're going to be removed from those scary statistics we talked about at the beginning of this introduction.

One more thing before we head into day one. Remember to make this book your own. Take the tools I'm giving you inside these pages and use them in a way that's right for you. That may mean going off independently and making your financial plan, or it may mean taking it to a financial planner and getting advice that's specific to your own personal situation. The goal here is to get you started on your journey—to help guide you toward your destination. While I can give you some tips along the way, I can't take the actual journey with you and I can't tell you how to personally climb each hill or deal with each obstacle.

Because the actual traveling part of the journey? That's all about you. So pack your gear, and let's get started!

Day 1

Your IRA

One of the simplest things you can do to prepare for retirement is to open an IRA. An IRA is an individual retirement account. These accounts are preferable to other savings accounts because they are considered qualified, which means they have tax incentives for people who are setting aside money for retirement. Those tax incentives not only save you money on taxes each year that you're contributing, they can also allow your savings to grow tax-deferred or tax-free and potentially remove tax burdens once you retire.

Choosing an IRA

There are many different factors to analyze when choosing an IRA, but let's start off simple. For employed individuals, the choice is between a Roth IRA or a Traditional IRA. With a Roth IRA, you may get little or no tax deduction for the funds you put in (depends on whether you qualify for the Saver's Credit, a special deduction offered by the IRS for people within a certain income bracket), but once you start taking qualified distributions, you can take them out tax-free. This means you never pay taxes on the growth of the contributions you make.

> ### What Is a Qualified Distribution?
> When you take a distribution from a tax-qualified account, and that distribution meets the added age and withdrawal rules, it's considered a qualified distribution and is, as a result, not subject to penalties. For some accounts, such as Roth IRAs, it also may not be subject to taxation.

With a Traditional IRA, you can get tax deductions for the amount you contribute (and some may also qualify for an added deduction through the Saver's Credit), but the amount of the deduction will depend on your income.[4] Your contributions will also grow without taxes, but they may be taxed at retirement when you begin taking distributions.

Now, even though I said you have to choose between the two, technically you can open one of each. However, you

---

[4] 2016 IRA Contribution and Deduction Limits
https://www.irs.gov/retirement-plans/plan-participant-employee/2016-ira-contribution-and-deduction-limits-effect-of-modified-agi-on-deductible-contributions-if-you-are-covered-by-a-retirement-plan-at-work

must remember that the annual contribution limits are cumulative. Therefore, you have to add together the contribution you make to the Traditional IRA and the contribution you make to the Roth and make sure that, combined, they don't exceed your annual contribution limit.

So, what is the IRA contribution limit? Well, for 2020, it's $6,000. That means you can contribute a cumulative total of $6,000 to your IRAs.[5] If you think it's best to have both a Traditional and a Roth, then however you decide to divide that contribution is up to you.

Roth and Traditional IRA account holders can contribute to their account their entire working life—even if that stretches into their seventies, eighties, and nineties.

Baby Boomers
Individuals who are fifty and over can make an added "catch-up" contribution of $1,000 per year.

Wait—That's Not All

That was the simplified version of the differences between Traditional and Roth IRAs. Now let's go a bit deeper and see what else we should consider before opening an account.

- Required minimum distributions (RMDs): During the year in which you turn 72, you're required to start taking a certain minimum distribution from your Traditional IRA. For many people, this isn't a

---

[5]For specific rules and limits based on marital, employment and filing status, please visit IRS.gov

problem since they plan to rely on the IRA for income at that age anyway. But for some who don't actually need to take the income, it can create a tax problem as the RMD will increase their income. Likewise, it can deplete the account (which is the intention of the minimum), making it difficult to pass anything on to heirs. The Roth IRA, on the other hand, has no such requirement.[6]

- Income limits: As of 2020, the Roth IRA only allows contributions from those who earn less than $139,000 per year ($205,999 for married couples filing jointly). There are ways to get around this with what's called a "backdoor Roth," which is also referred to as a conversion or recharacterization, but you must get professional help if you want to avoid accidentally creating large tax ramifications for yourself. Since this book is focused on simplifying the retirement planning process, I'm not going to go into detail about this process here.

Tax-Deferred versus Tax-Free

While you don't technically have to choose between going the tax-free route with a Roth or the tax-deferred route with a Traditional, it's still important to think about which might benefit you the most so that, even if you open one of each, you can divide your contribution according to priority.

---

[6]IRA Required Minimum Distribution Worksheet, https://www.irs.gov/pub/irs-tege/uniform_rmd_wksht.pdf

Using a tax-deferred retirement account means getting a tax deduction on contributions, which can help you pay off debt and reach other financial goals. Once you retire and begin taking out distributions, however, not only are those distributions taxable, but they also increase your overall income. This may impact whether your Social Security payments are subject to federal income tax. Because distributions from a Roth are not taxable, they would have no impact on the taxability of your Social Security income.

Solutions for the Self-Employed

Self-employed individuals must be especially careful about retirement planning because there is no employer plan to back them up. Instead, they're completely responsible for picking their plan and funding it. Self-employed individuals also have the added burden of covering their full Social Security and Medicare taxes, something that would normally be halved with their employer.

When it comes to IRAs, the self-employed have two popular choices: they can open a Simplified Employee Pension (SEP) IRA or a Savings Incentive Match Plan for Employees (SIMPLE) IRA. Let's explore the differences between the two:

- SEP IRA: One of the biggest benefits of a SEP is that it has a higher contribution limit than a SIMPLE. As of 2020, self-employed individuals could contribute a maximum of 25 percent of their net pay, or $57,000 (whichever was larger). A drawback, however, is that individuals with employees may be required to offer this benefit to their qualified employees and since the owner is the only contributor, that can create a large financial burden.

- SIMPLE IRA: SIMPLE IRAs have lower contribution limits ($13,500 under 50 and $16,500 if over 50 in 2020)[7], but employer contributions are limited to 3 percent of the employee's contribution, so when a self-employed individual has qualifying employees they must offer the plan to, it can help limit their expenses.

Millennials

At the beginning of your career, when your income is lower and you still have student loan interest deductions, it could be a good time to contribute to a Roth. You can then switch to a Traditional as your income rises and you can better benefit from the deduction. Then, at retirement, you'll have access to both tax-free income and tax-deferred growth.

Opening the IRA

Once you've decided which IRA(s) might best fit your future plans, it's time to open the account. IRAs are held by

---

[7] For full discussion on limits, please visit the IRS page at: https://www.irs.gov/retirement-plans/plan-participant-employee/retirement-topics-simple-ira-contribution-limits

custodians such as insurance companies, banks, and financial brokerage firms. Before filling out the documents and choosing your custodian, there are several things you want to compare:

- Is there an annual fee for having the account?
- What are the commissions? Are they flat and affordable?
- How many mutual fund families will you have access to? Are there many load-free choices (this concept is explained in more detail on Day 4)?
- What kind of investments might you want to make? Depending on the custodian you choose, you might be able to buy stocks, bonds, mutual funds, CDs, annuities, precious metals, and even real estate trusts.

Day 1 Checklist

☐ Think about which kind of IRA is going to be best for your retirement objectives.
☐ Choose a custodian you think will give you the investment options you need.
☐ Open the IRA(s).

Day 2

Your Company 401(k)

If your employer wanted to give you some extra money each year, would you turn it down? Would you tell them that you aren't interested in getting any additional money from them? This may sound like a crazy thing to even suggest, but if you're not contributing to your company-sponsored 401(k), that is essentially what you're doing.

The Value of the Employer Match

Many employers who offer their employees a 401(k) do what's called a "company match." Through this, they match a percentage of their employees' contributions. Some companies might offer a straight 100 percent match of employee contributions up to a set limit (say, 3 percent) while others match a percentage of their employees' contributions (for example, matching 50 percent of an employee's first 10 percent contributed). Whichever method your company employs, if it offers a match, then it's essentially turning down free money if you don't take advantage of it.

Not only do employer matches add up to potentially thousands or tens of thousands of extra dollars over the decades you receive them, but they are also invested within the 401(k) (something discussed in more detail later in this chapter). That means that they can grow if your 401(k) performs well, and that they can help absorb or lessen some of the losses to your own principal contributed.

Open Enrollment

A 401(k) isn't something you can just sign up for anytime (unless you're new to the company and just now qualified to take part). Instead, you generally have to wait for open enrollment. So today, you want to start by finding out when your company's open enrollment is. That way you can set an appointment in your phone or on your calendar to make sure you enroll by that date.

What's the Match?

Earlier we talked about how important it is to get as much of your employer match as you can afford—which is determined by how much of your income you must contribute to earn it. When you make your 401(k) elections, you will tell the benefits administrator how much you want withheld from each paycheck for your 401(k) contribution. Essentially, you want to at least withhold whatever it takes to get the maximum employer match. For example, let's say your employer matches 100 percent of your first 3 percent of contributions. If you're making $40,000 per year, then that means you want to contribute at least $1,200 per year. Then, your employer will also chip in the same amount, effectively doubling your contributions. Let's say you make $40,000 and your employer matches 50 percent of your first 6 percent of contributions. In that case, if you contribute $1,200 a year, your employer will contribute $600. To max it out and get the employer's full contribution match, then you must contribute $2,400 a year.

By maxing out a contribution[8] to at least get your full employer match, you're making sure you take in all the extra money you're entitled to.

Baby Boomers
Individuals who are fifty and over can make added annual "catch-up" 401(k) contributions. In 2020 the allowable 401(k) catch-up amount was $6,500.

401(k) Options for the Self-Employed

When you own a business where the owner-employee is the only employee, then you can consider implementing a Solo 401(k). With a Solo 401(k), self-employed individuals can defer a portion of their income into the plan each year. The

---

[8]You can see the IRS contribution limits for 401(k)s here: https://www.irs.gov/retirement-plans/plan-participant-employee/retirement-topics-401k-and-profit-sharing-plan-contribution-limits

limit, which was $19,500 for individuals under fifty in 2020, is still applicable, even if it's equal to the individual's total income.

Further, the owner-employee can elect to have the business contribute up to 25 percent of the owner's income. Solo 401(k)s do have total contribution limits, so you should check with the IRS annually to see what those are.[9]

401(k) Investing Options

401(k) plans are different from IRAs in that these accounts generally don't allow you to invest in individual stocks and bonds, but you may have the opportunity to buy company stock, sometimes at a discount. Whether it's through an employee stock purchase plan (ESPP) or stock options, this can give you a great opportunity to make an advantageous purchase of company stock at a lower price than it's trading for in the market.

There are things you must consider before investing in company stock, however. First, you need to focus on diversifying your holdings and avoiding being too heavily invested in the company. Instead, diversify between company stock and the other investment options allowed (explained in more detail on the next page). This is a lesson that was learned by employees of the company Enron, many of whom lost a large portion (if not all) of their retirement

---

[9]One-Participant 401(k) Plans, https://www.irs.gov/retirement-plans/one-participant-401k-plans

savings in 2001 when the stock price fell almost 94 percent and the company ended up bankrupt.[10]

Another consideration you must make before investing in company stock is to understand how your options and stock purchase plan will be affected if you leave the company. For this, you need to contact human resources and get all the details.

Outside company stock investing, you also have the option of investing in various mutual funds within your 401(k). These funds invest in a variety of underlying assets such as bonds, stocks, and fixed investments. Not only does this allow for some diversification of underlying assets but you can also diversify even more by choosing multiple funds. For example, you could invest part of your savings in international funds, some in equity funds, and a portion in an income fund.

Spreading your risk in this way can help you reduce your potential for loss, allow you to take advantage of market moves and growth within a specific sector, and help you secure your retirement.

Vesting Vitals

While any money you contribute to your 401(k) is yours from day one, the money your employer contributes or matches isn't necessarily yours until you've met the employer's vesting requirements. Vesting is the process of tying ownership to the number of years worked. Some

---

[10]The New York Times, 2001,
http://www.nytimes.com/2001/11/22/business/employees-retirement-plan-is-a-victim-as-enron-tumbles.html

employers choose a graduated vesting schedule, allowing employees to vest by a certain percentage every few years. Others require a set number of years for 100 percent vesting—and nothing in between.

So why does this matter? Consider this: let's say that in five years, your employer (Employer A) considers you 50 percent vested. That means that if you switch jobs five years after you start contributing to Employer A's 401(k), then you can take 50 percent of Employer A's contributions with you and roll them over to a new company 401(k). But if you leave just a couple of months short of this deadline, you will forfeit all of Employer A's contributions. Knowing the vesting information helps you make informed decisions in the future so you can retain as much of that money as possible.

Millennials

Research has found that millennials generally expect to stay in one job for less than 3 years—which means they often miss out on full vesting. Pay attention to your employer's partial vesting schedule and see if you can plan your job hunt around those periods. Even if you can't, a 401(k) is still a great way to gain tax-deferred growth with managed funds.

To Roll or Not to Roll

When you leave one employer for another, you may be able to roll your 401(k) assets into your new employer's 401(k) or into an IRA.[11] While there's a lot to consider when making this decision, one thing to keep in mind is that while both Traditional IRAs and 401(k)s have required minimum distributions (RMDs) beginning in the year you turn 72, you can get around this requirement if you continue working and contributing to the 401(k) offered by your current employer. In other words, if you are still working at age 72, you won't have to take an RMD from the 401(k) that you still contribute to. If, however, you've rolled an ex-employer's 401(k) assets into an IRA, you will be required to take distributions from those funds, which can increase your overall taxable income.

If your new employer doesn't allow rollovers or doesn't have a 401(k), then your best option is to roll over into an IRA. Otherwise, if you leave the funds with your former employer, you could easily forget them and allow them to languish without ongoing management.

When you roll a 401(k) into an IRA, the funds go to another financial institution and you may have a new variety of financial products to invest in. Some of these may allow you to create a guaranteed minimum income stream that's guaranteed for life. This income stream could supplement other retirement benefits, so considering a rollover to an IRA can be advantageous at the right time.

---

[11]You can also choose to take an early distribution, but taxes and penalties generally make this a bad idea.

Speaking of rolling into an IRA at the right time, RMDs from 401(k)s are subject to a mandated 20 percent withholding for federal taxation. There is no mandated withholding from an IRA, so rolling over your 401(k) assets to an IRA prior to retirement can allow you to eliminate the withholding and instead pay taxes when you file annually.

Gen X

It's not shocking to imagine the majority of gen Xers working well into their 70s. If they do, then required minimum distributions could force them to make large tax payments that are completely unnecessary.

Day 2 Checklist

☐ Find out when open enrollment is.
☐ Determine what you need to contribute to get the max employer match.
☐ Learn about vesting.
☐ Research investment options.

Day 3

Your Investing Plan

Now that you're saving money in your retirement accounts, it's time to start thinking about creating an investment plan.

Please note, I am not suggesting that you go it alone and start investing after today. Whether you choose to work with a financial planner, a financial advisor, or a robo-advisor, it's always best to get some professional guidance from those who specialize in this area. However, before meeting with an advisor, take time to build your knowledge about investing.

Understanding Risk

There are two types of risk you need to evaluate when it comes to investing: your personal risk, and the risk of various investments.

Personal Risk Tolerance

How comfortable are you with the concept of losing money? That's the fundamental question you must answer to determine your personal risk tolerance. For some, the idea of a financial loss isn't scary—especially when it's tied to the potential for a high return. For others, the idea of loss makes them feel sick and scared—and no amount of potential gain helps them feel better about it.

The less comfortable you are with the potential for loss, the lower your risk tolerance is and the less risky your investments should be.

Some of the questions you need to ask yourself when assessing your risk tolerance include:

- When do you need the money? The sooner you plan to use it, the less risk you should want to take on.
- Which is more important to you—avoiding risk or beating inflation? The higher a return you want to earn, the more risk you are likely to take on.
- If you lost 20 percent of your portfolio's value, how would it make you feel? The market is volatile. If this kind of loss makes you uncomfortable, then you might have a lower tolerance for risk.

> **Millennials**
>
> Don't assume that just because you're young, you should be comfortable with aggressive, high-risk investments. Instead, measure your actual attitude toward risk and allow that to point you in the right direction.

Investment Risk

Once you've determined your personal risk tolerance, you will be shown different investments that will meet that tolerance level. Each of the investments you're shown, however, will have its own unique type of risk attached to it that you also must evaluate and decide whether it's suitable for you. For example, let's say you believe that interest rates are going to go up. The interest rate risk attached to a bond issued today, at a low rate, could be unacceptable to you. In that case, you may want to stick with short-term bonds and CDs rather than long-term issues. Some of the investment risks you need to be aware of include:

- Market risk: The risk of losses due to market volatility.
- Interest rate risk: The risk that a bond or CD you own will lose value as interest rates on new issues rise.
- Liquidity risk: The risk that you will not be able to sell your investments quickly enough to get access to cash when you need it.

- Reinvestment risk: The risk that you may not be able to reinvest funds from matured bonds and CDs at as high a rate as they were earning in the older issues.

Investing for Income

The point of investing within your retirement account isn't just to grow the money but also to find investments that throw off an income. Some of the options you have for income-producing investments include:

- Dividend-paying stocks: Dividend stocks can both appreciate in per-share value and provide income through dividends. Remember, however, that dividends aren't guaranteed and that these positions can still suffer from swings in the stock market.
- Mutual funds: There are many funds that invest in bonds allowing the funds to issue regular dividend income. Be careful of high expense ratios (which are annual fees charged as a percentage of assets to cover fund expenses) and the quality of the underlying securities. Some of these bond funds even focus on tax-exempt, government-issued bonds called municipal bonds, allowing you to invest in them within your nonqualified accounts and still get a tax benefit. You can also consider target-date retirement income funds, in which the asset managers shift the funds' asset class to highlight income risk management as you get closer to your chosen target date (retirement).
- Bonds: Buying individual bonds can allow you to gain income until maturity. Look for highly rated

bonds and consider alternating (or laddering) the maturity dates so that you can shield yourself from interest rate risks.

- Annuities: These are contracts issued by life insurance companies that can be designed to have a rider, called a guaranteed minimum income benefit (GMIB), that guarantees a stable income for your entire life, no matter how the market is performing. Annuities have a lot of flexibility in design so not only can they protect you from drops in the market, they can also help pay for long-term care and final expenses, making them a very popular income planning vehicle.

Meeting Rebalancing Needs

Once you invest your money, you can't just leave it on its own. You have to schedule time each year to potentially rebalance your accounts. Remember that some of your investments will grow in value and some will drop, and this will change the overall asset allocation and risk suitability within your portfolio, making rebalancing vital for keeping your portfolio focused the way you want it to be. Additionally, as you age you are likely to have a gradually reducing risk tolerance, and your investments will need to be adjusted to reflect that.

As mentioned earlier, target-date funds can be an excellent means to achieving monitored, professional rebalancing based on the chosen "target" date.

Day 3 Checklist

☐ Assess your personal level of investment risk.
☐ Learn about the various risks presented by the investments you are considering.
☐ Research target date funds to see if any fit your needs.

Day 4

Your Investment Options

While your first step is to deposit funds regularly into your 401(k), IRAs, and personal savings accounts, your next step is to decide what to then *do* with those funds once they're deposited. That means researching your various investment options.

401(k) Options Reviewed

As discussed on Day 2, you have multiple options available to invest within your 401(k). You can divide up your contributions among multiple funds to help distribute risk and capitalize on the movement within a variety of markets. You may also be able to buy company stock, sometimes at a discount. It's important that you understand the dynamics of each of the funds available to you so that you get a sense of what types of economic events might affect each of them and how they complement each other within a portfolio. You also need to understand their level of risk and consider how that matches your own age and risk tolerance.

The investing options within a 401(k) are pretty restrictive, however. That's why some people, upon leaving an employer, choose to roll their 401(k) over to an IRA where they can invest in a broader variety of products, including those that provide a guaranteed income for life.

Rollovers or Transfers?

Throughout this book, I talk about both rollovers and transfers for IRAs. Right now, I'd like to discuss the difference between these two moves.

Transfer: When you are able to have assets moved directly from one plan to another (from trustee to trustee or custodian to custodian), then you are doing a transfer. Transfers will help you avoid any potential tax issues or penalties.

Rollover: When a direct transfer from trustee to trustee isn't done, then you will receive the assets from one plan and will have sixty days to roll them into a new plan to avoid taxes and penalties. While a transfer can be done as many times as necessary, rollovers can only be done once per year.

It's vital that, when leaving one job where you have a 401(k), you make immediate plans to either transfer the

401(k) to your new company's plan or into an IRA. If you don't, it's very possible you could forget the account and be subject to losses and fees as a result of leaving it unmanaged. This, sadly, happens all the time. I have a client who recently retired and left $1.4 million in a 401(k). He forgot all about the account and when the market fell, he lost 20 percent of his account value. This could have been prevented, if he had only transferred or rolled over those funds. If you're close to retirement, you may even want to consider in-service withdrawals, if your employer has that provision. This would allow you to move a portion of your funds out of risk, move funds into an IRA, and even enjoy some tax benefits.

IRA Options

An IRA is a fairly flexible account type and most of the restrictions regarding investment options will depend on the custodian you choose. For example, some custodians may allow for the investment of physical assets, such as precious metals, while others may not. Some may permit certain mutual fund families that others don't.

While the flexibility of IRA investing options is certainly appealing, it's also a double-edged sword. With so many choices—from annuities with guaranteed income for life to stocks with tremendous growth potential (and loss possibilities), to mutual funds and real estate investment trusts—investors have an almost overwhelming number of choices facing them, and that can be intimidating.

It's obviously impossible to give specific advice in a book like this, so I'll say two things: first, don't rush into anything. Give yourself the freedom to research and understand the benefits, pitfalls, and very real risks of all the potential investments you're considering. Second, don't be afraid to ask for help. Financial advisors are there to help you better understand the investing world. After all, it's what they spend their entire career doing. In some cases, for those who are just starting out, you may even find that new automated, algorithm-based financial management and investment systems, called robo-advisors, offer you some guidance in choosing appropriate investments.

Lastly, remember that no matter what you choose to invest in, every single investment has risks—many of which were discussed in the last chapter. Even fixed investments have certain risks. Make sure you fully understand the risks involved in the investments you choose and that they make sense for your risk tolerance, timeline, and goals. You also need to make sure that your accounts are diversified among different types of investments with varying types of risks.

Personal Savings Accounts

The investment decisions you make for your personal savings will depend a lot on the intentions you have for that money. For example, your emergency funds should probably be kept in an easy-to-liquidate money market account or similar investment. Savings intended for future goals might be better suited for stocks, bonds, CDs, and mutual funds. Because personal savings is usually intended for use well before retirement, remember to factor in any potential early liquidation penalties you could face with certain investments. Strategies such as CD ladders, where you split up your savings into several CDs with varying maturity dates, can help with this.

Baby Boomers

Don't forget to take advantage of the added $1,000 you can contribute to an IRA and $6,500 you can contribute to a 401(k) for catch-up contributions when you are fifty or older.

General Tips

- When reviewing the various investment options available for your accounts, it's important to consider the risk involved. While some more aggressive risk can afford you higher returns, it also increases your risk of loss—and you have to think about whether you can afford to take a loss and how comfortable you are knowing that it's possible.
- Another consideration is the way you want to earn money from your investments. For example, if you are getting close to retirement and want to start taking distributions from your account, you may want to focus on investments that provide some income, such as dividend stocks, bonds, and annuities.
- Always make sure you understand the various fees involved in making transactions in your account. While annuities often get a bad rap for having fees, many people don't realize that fixed annuities (including index annuities) don't have fees unless

certain options are added to them—such as guaranteed income riders. Variable annuities, in which you choose subaccounts with a variety of stock and bond investments, have fees—mortality fees, investment management fees, and annual maintenance fees. These types of annuities are risky and should be avoided by people who are risk and/or fee conscious. It's also important to remember that annuities aren't the only retirement saving option with fees. For example, stocks have commissions for both purchase and sale, and mutual funds have management fees as well as often having charges upon purchase and sale (called front-end and back-end loads). So always be aware of the fees, what you're getting in exchange for them, and how they will impact the money you have available to invest.

Day 4 Checklist

☐ Learn about 401(k) investment options.
☐ Research various types of investments that have different kinds of risks.
☐ Make sure you understand the various fees in your accounts and investments.

Day 5

Your Insurance Review

The goal of insurance varies depending on the types of policies you have. Some policies, such as home insurance, are meant to make you whole after losing property or enduring damage during an insurable incident. Others, such as liability insurance, protect you against the cost of damages that you could accidentally cause. Still other types of insurance, such as disability, replace lost income. Whether you realize it or not, insurance is one of the most important ways for you to protect your assets and preserve your income.

One of the great things about insurance is that there are so many different types to choose from, all of which are tailored to protecting your specific situation and assets. Some of the most common products are property and casualty products, which includes home and flood insurance, liability insurance, auto insurance, renters' insurance, and umbrella policies for added protection.

There's no question that working with a local agent and getting insurance is critical to your overall financial success, but once you get your policies, it's important to review them regularly, which means at least on an annual basis.

What are you looking for during this review? The basics you want to check for are:

- proper limits
- practicality of deductibles
- appropriateness of coverage
- fair terms
- company ratings
- affordable premiums

Let's take a look at each of these factors in more detail.

Proper Limits

While it's important to ensure that your limits are high enough to actually make you whole after suffering losses through an insurable incident, you also want to make sure that your limits aren't too high. Overinsuring your property leads to high premiums for nothing, as your claims are still likely to be processed only at the actual amount of the loss.

Practicality of Deductibles

Your insurance deductibles represent the amount you must pay out of your own pocket, or savings, in order to cover damages and losses after covered incidents. Because this money comes out of your personal funds, it's important to review your deductibles every year to ensure you can reasonably expect to pay them. Higher deductibles will generally reduce your premiums, but if you aren't setting some of those savings aside to actually help you cover the deductibles, then you could be sabotaging your savings.

It's also worth considering that some insurable incidents can impact multiple lines of coverage at once—such as the house fire that totals your home, boat, and car. This will prompt multiple deductible payments that you might not be prepared to pay.

Lastly, make sure you understand which deductibles are per year and which are per incident. If a policy has a $1,000 annual deductible, it means that this is the most you will pay for the entire year, in terms of deductibles. But if a policy has a $1,000 deductible per incident, it means you could be paying as much as $1,000 every time you have a claim.

Appropriateness of Coverage

These days, the lines between business and personal use of property is increasingly blurred. If you make money on social media from home, does that mean you need commercial liability coverage on your home? If you drive part time for Uber or Lyft, do you need commercial car insurance? If you bring your tablet to the local coffee shop to finish work for clients, do you need commercial insurance on the tablet? What about the car that you drove to get to the coffee shop? Working with an agent and explaining how you use your property will help sort out what the appropriate type of coverage is for you.

Fair/Reasonable Terms

When you sit down and read your insurance policies—wait, are you saying you haven't done that? Okay, probably very few people have, but all of us should. Policies have different terms that may or may not fulfill your expectations. As an example, a home insurance policy may pay for replacement of your damaged items, or it may only reimburse you for their fair market value, which means you get the depreciated value of the item you had—and this may be less than you actually need in order to replace it.

You have to understand each of these terms in order to decide whether the benefits in your policy are set up to give you the most value.

Company Ratings

A. M. Best consistently reviews insurance carriers to make sure they can handle the financial burden of potential claims. While a carrier may get a high rating one year—say, the year you decide to buy a policy through them—another year they may get a very different, lower rating. It's important to review the A. M. Best ratings of all your insurance companies annually to make sure they are still in a position to make good on any claims you might have.

Affordable Premiums

Premiums are, in part, based on the insurance company's assessment of the risks you present. These risks can change depending on your age, marital status, and so on. In some cases, you may even qualify for various discounts as your need for insurance grows. Many people don't realize that you can get discounts for bundling policies, for maintaining a clean driving record, for completing various driving courses, agreeing to certain electronic monitoring, and more. Each year, you should work with your agent to ensure that you are getting the most affordable premiums and that you aren't missing out on any discounts.

Day 5 Checklist

☐ Evaluate all your insurance policies for:
- proper limits
- practicality of deductibles
- appropriateness of coverage
- fair terms
- company ratings
- affordable premiums

Day 6

Your Life Insurance

People buy life insurance for a variety of reasons. Business owners can use these policies to fund their buy-sell agreements or to provide needed cash when they lose a key employee. Families buy life insurance to provide ongoing income for a family when it loses its breadwinner. Parents buy life insurance to ensure their children will have funds to go to college even if one of the parents passes away. Spouses buy life insurance to ensure that debts, such as mortgages, can be paid off even after the loss of a spouse.

Life insurance isn't just part of a thorough estate plan, it's also part of a secure *retirement* plan. When properly designed and used, a life insurance policy can provide unique, tax-favored benefits to retirees while also helping them save money on a variety of expenses, including long-term care protection.

Life Policy Basics

There are three basic types of life insurance:

- Term life: An inexpensive policy designed to offer coverage for a limited period of time. Can often be converted to a whole life policy.
- Whole life: A policy that accrues cash values and is designed to offer coverage over your lifetime. Whole life policies feature fixed, guaranteed premiums and guaranteed death benefits.
- Universal life: A type of permanent life policy with flexible premiums and options for cash value growth. Can be a helpful planning tool.

Millennials

If your parents cosigned for your student loans, they may be liable to pay them back after you pass away. Life insurance can help you protect them.

Each of these life insurance policies has a different role to play in both death benefit and retirement benefits. When it comes to retirement benefits, life policies can ensure that your spouse has enough money to retire even if they lose you at an early age (and vice versa). It can also be a source of funds to tap into for tax-free loans.

Evaluating Your Life Insurance

Your current life insurance policies may already have the very benefits you want and need in order to enhance your retirement. When you review your existing life insurance policies, there are a few things you need to look for. This includes:

- Adequacy of death benefit: Is it enough for your family to pay off debts and live and retire comfortably? The general rule of thumb is to have a policy worth seven to ten times your income.
- Potential for retirement income supplement: Most permanent life policies offer the opportunity for guaranteed cash value growth, creating a fund that you can borrow from when you need a loan but don't want to pay personal credit card and bank loan rates. Does your policy earn cash values that you can borrow from, without taxation?
- Additional benefits: Does your policy include any special riders to help pay for long-term care expenses or to advance the death benefit in the event of a terminal illness?

Gen X

If you bought a term policy earlier in life, now may be a good time to look into converting it to a permanent policy.

If you don't currently have life insurance coverage, there's no question that it's something you need to look into. Even as a millennial with no family or spouse, locking in cheaper premium rates now can be vital to how you plan to use the policy in the future. With a policy like indexed universal life insurance, you can benefit from gains in the market while still enjoying flexible premiums that allow you to pay higher premiums in good years and lower premiums in lean years, all without risking the illustrated cash value build-up (provided you pay minimums). This can give you access to money for college—for yourself or your children—through cash value gains. It's also not includable for FAFSA applications.

If, instead, you choose a term policy, you have the ability to convert that to a whole life policy later in life.

Life Insurance in Your Retirement Plan

Earlier in this book, I talked about the benefits of mailbox money—that lifetime income you get every month for life after you've retired. A whole or permanent life insurance policy can help you create a dependable source of mailbox money because these policies accrue cash values, which can be borrowed against without taxation under current IRS rules. Take a look at the life insurance illustration on the next page to see how the cash value fund accumulates to offer a potential source of income.

SAMPLE LIFE INSURANCE ILLUSTRATION

| | | | | | NON-GUARANTEED VALUES | | | | | |
| | | | | | 3.75% alternative crediting rate and current charges | | | Using illustrated crediting rates and current charges | | |
Year	Age	Premium outlay	Policy loan	Net outlay	Accumulation value	Surrender value	Death benefit	Accumulation value	Surrender value	Death benefit
1	35	$2,488	$0	$2,488	$1,989	$0	$102,026	$1,995	$0	$102,026
2	36	$2,488	$0	$2,488	$4,121	$2,041	$104,121	$4,268	$2,187	$104,268
3	37	$2,488	$0	$2,488	$6,266	$4,185	$106,266	$6,568	$4,488	$106,568
4	38	$2,488	$0	$2,488	$8,551	$6,470	$108,551	$9,163	$7,083	$109,163
5	39	$2,488	$0	$2,488	$10,855	$8,774	$110,855	$11,801	$9,721	$111,801
		$12,438								
6	40	$2,488	$0	$2,488	$13,304	$11,640	$113,304	$14,787	$13,103	$114,787
7	41	$2,488	$0	$2,488	$15,777	$14,529	$115,777	$17,790	$16,542	$117,790
8	42	$2,488	$0	$2,488	$18,400	$17,568	$118,400	$21,177	$20,345	$121,177
9	43	$2,488	$0	$2,488	$21,048	$20,632	$121,048	$24,634	$24,218	$124,634
10	44	$2,488	$0	$2,488	$23,852	$23,852	$123,852	$28,501	$28,501	$128,501
		$24,875								
11	45	$2,488	$0	$2,488	$26,963	$26,963	$126,963	$32,797	$32,797	$132,797
12	46	$2,488	$0	$2,488	$30,255	$30,255	$130,255	$37,599	$37,599	$137,599
13	47	$2,488	$0	$2,468	$33,592	$33,592	$133,592	$42,550	$42,550	$142,550
14	48	$2,488	$0	$2,488	$37,127	$37,127	$137,127	$48,087	$48,087	$148,087
15	49	$2,488	$0	$2,488	$40,716	$40,716	$140,716	$53,807	$53,807	$153,807
		$37,313								
16	50	$2,488	$0	$2,488	$44,513	$44,513	$144,513	$60,197	$60,197	$160,197
17	51	$2,488	$0	$2,488	$48,365	$48,365	$148,365	$66,797	$66,797	$166,797
18	52	$2,488	$0	$2,488	$52,433	$52,433	$152,433	$74,161	$74,161	$174,161
19	53	$2,488	$0	$2,488	$56,554	$56,554	$156,554	$81,766	$81,766	$181,766
20	54	$2,488	$0	$2,488	$60,901	$60,901	$160,901	$90,244	$90,244	$190,244

| | | | | | NON-GUARANTEED VALUES | | | | | |
| | | | | | 3.75% alternative crediting rate and current charges | | | Using illustrated crediting rates and current charges | | |
Year	Age	Premium outlay	Policy loan	Net outlay	Accumulation value	Surrender value	Death benefit	Accumulation value	Surrender value	Death benefit
21	55	$2,488	$0	$2,488	$65,293	$65,293	$165,293	$98,994	$98,994	$198,994
22	56	$2,488	$0	$2,488	$69,922	$69,922	$169,922	$108,743	$108,743	$208,743
23	57	$2,488	$0	$2,488	$74,597	$74,597	$174,597	$118,809	$118,809	$218,809
24	58	$2,488	$0	$2,488	$79,530	$79,530	$179,530	$130,029	$130,029	$230,029
25	59	$2,488	$0	$2,488	$84,517	$84,517	$184,517	$141,625	$141,625	$241,625
		$62,188								
26	60	$2,488	$0	$2,488	$89,767	$89,767	$189,767	$154,537	$154,537	$254,537
27	61	$2,488	$0	$2,488	$95,060	$95,060	$195,060	$167,875	$167,875	$267,875
28	62	$2,488	$0	$2,488	$100,615	$100,615	$200,615	$182,707	$182,707	$282,707
29	63	$2,488	$0	$2,488	$106,198	$106,198	$206,198	$198,021	$198,021	$298,021
30	64	$2,488	$0	$2,488	$112,051	$112,051	$212,051 #	$215,043	$215,043	$315,043 #
		$74,625								

FIGURE 1
SAMPLE MALE, AGE 35, $100,000 DEATH BENEFIT, NONSMOKER. SAMPLE ONLY. NOT A GUARANTEE OF PERFORMANCE.

Making Adjustments to Insurance

A life insurance agent can help you go through your existing policy and make sure that it's designed to meet all your current and future needs. They can also help you add additional policies, such as term insurance, to increase the death benefit at a lower cost.

A life agent can also help you choose an insurance company with the financial strength to rely on, well into the future.

Day 6 Checklist

- [ ] Learn what type of life policy you have.
- [ ] Determine whether the death benefit is sufficient.
- [ ] Find out whether there is cash value accrual.
- [ ] Find out what added benefits the policy has.

Day 7

Your Preretirement Budget

So far, we've talked a bit about savings, but we haven't explored how to decide what you can afford to put into these accounts. For that, you need to create a budget.

While it's true the focus of this book is on your money *after* retirement, it's your *pre*retirement financial management that will dictate how much you can afford to save for that far-off (or near) retirement date. Managing your money <u>now</u> means you'll have more to set aside for later, which makes your preretirement budget an absolute priority.

Starting Your Budget

The process of budgeting may not be as difficult as you think. In fact, getting started with one is extremely easy. At their core, budgets are all about preserving as much of your income as possible—so that's where you start, with your income.

You need to consider your guaranteed income from all sources. That means child support payments, disability payments, work income, and interest payments. You can also add in your expected (but not guaranteed) income such as bonuses and commissions, although this income will be treated differently.

Generally, you want to break your income down into a monthly number. If you want tighter control, you can go weekly, but monthly can make things easier. To get that monthly number, you want to be as exact as possible. That means that you shouldn't take a weekly income and multiply it by four. Instead, you should multiply your weekly income by fifty-two pay periods and then divide it by twelve. Likewise, a salary that's paid biweekly shouldn't be multiplied by two to get the monthly amount, but should be multiplied by the twenty-six pay periods in a year and then divided by twelve.

The Second Step

A budget represents an accounting of your income minus your expenses. So after you've added up your income, it's time to list your expenses. Some of your expenses, especially those that are discretionary, may be harder to define than your static expenses, such as utilities, mortgage, rent, and car payments. For discretionary (or optional) spending, such as groceries, dining out, clothing, personal care, and entertainment, you should take out your credit card and bank statements and add up the average amount spent over the past six months.

Remember, your budget needs to account for <u>all</u> of your income and <u>all</u> of your spending. You can't gloss over or ignore any of the spending patterns you have.

Making Adjustments

After subtracting your expenses from your guaranteed income, you will either find that you make enough money to support all of your expenses, or you don't. It's pretty obvious if you don't that you need to go through and make adjustments that allow you to actually afford all your bills and, eventually, savings. But even if your expenses are less than your income, you still need to go through your spending trends and see if there are areas you can reduce because in future chapters, I'm going to talk about making savings contributions—and you'll need to have room in your budget to do this. Expenses to watch for that can be reduced include:

- Unnecessary monthly subscription fees: This can include digital or paper magazines, newspapers, streaming services, and more.
- Cell phone data plans
- Overspending on prepared and delivered foods: This can include restaurant dining, delivery and takeout, as well as services such as Plated and Blue Apron.

- High grocery bills, including grocery delivery fees
- Monthly services you can handle yourself, such as home and lawn maintenance
- App spending
- Music downloads
- Individual streaming content rentals and purchases
- Excessive personal care, including a high number of annual hair, nail, and facial or skin care appointments

When cutting these expenses, use your guaranteed income as a guide. Extra, anticipated income can help you with unexpected expenses and can increase your savings, but it should not be counted on to pay for average monthly expenses.

By the end of this process, you'll end up with two budgets: the one you've actually been following and the more ideal one that you need to start using.

Baby Boomers

Even if you're just a few years away from retirement, it's still important to have a budget for your spending. Not only can it help you avoid taking on debt right before you leave work, it can ensure you keep your savings on track.

Increasing Cash Flow after Fifty

The goal in changing your spending is to increase the amount of money you have to put toward important, impactful actions such as saving. As you age, increases in cash flow will more often come from cuts in spending rather than taking on extra side work. One method many seniors use to increase cash flow after age fifty is by downsizing. Not only does this move increase cash flow before retirement so that debt and savings can be the main spending focus, it also helps the senior reduce their future postretirement income needs, which makes them less reliant on savings withdrawals.

Reducing Debt

While your budget is likely going to focus on increasing your savings, it's also important to find a way to more aggressively pay off debt. Not only do you want to be debt-free by the time you hit retirement, but you want to limit the amount of money you waste on paying interest in order to maintain long-term debts. For some, debt consolidation may offer the perfect way to aggressively reduce debt, by reworking balances and interest and creating a single monthly payment.

Discipline Is Key

It's probably safe to say that very few people enjoy the task of budgeting. It forces us to take an honest look at our finances and our spending. But another reason is that it requires us to follow our own rules and restrict our spending. If you aren't disciplined, your budget won't work.

Essentially, when it comes to budgets, you are the only obstacle to success.

Personal Budget

Monthly Income

INCOME SOURCES	AMOUNT
Income Source 1	
Income Source 2	
Other	

Monthly Expenses

ITEM	HISTORICAL	BUDGETED ADJUSTMENT
Rent/mortgage		
Electricity		
Property taxes		
Property/renters' insurance		
Repairs/maintenance		
Water and sewer		
Cable		
Other		
Cell phone		
Groceries		
Dining out		
Car payment		
Auto expenses		
Gas		
Auto insurance		
Student loans		
Personal loans/installment		
Credit cards		
Health insurance		
Life, disability, LTC insurance		

The 30-Day Retirement Plan

Monthly Expenses

ITEM	HISTORICAL	BUDGETED ADJUSTMENT
Child care		
Charitable contributions		
Personal care		
Clothing		
Entertainment		
Miscellaneous		

Monthly Savings

ACCOUNT TYPE	HISTORICAL	BUDGETED
IRA		
401(k)		
Nonqualified		

TOTAL MONTHLY INCOME

TOTAL MONTHLY EXPENSES

TOTAL MONTHLY SAVINGS

CASH BALANCE

Day 7 Checklist

☐ Use the budget worksheets on the previous pages, or another budgeting tool, to create your budget.

☐ Start implementing changes in your lifestyle and spending so you can live within your budget.

Day 8

Your Retirement Savings Contributions

With a fully prepared budget, it's now time to commit to regular IRA contributions, 401(k) contributions, and contributions to any other qualified account you have access to.

What Can You Afford to Contribute?

The first step in making retirement savings contributions is deciding how much money you can afford to deposit each month or week into your various savings accounts. For this, you'll need to review the budget you made yesterday.

Your first priority is generally to maximize any employer benefits you get. That means taking advantage of matches they offer for 401(k) contributions and taking some advantage of discounted company stock purchases. These can help you quickly accelerate your overall savings. Let's look at a couple examples.

EMPLOYEE STOCK PURCHASE

Market price for 100 shares	$3,500
Employee price for 100 shares	$2,500
Gain	$1,000

FIGURE 2

401(K) MATCH EXAMPLE

401(k) Growth of Contributions			
Year	Employee Contribution	Employer Contribution	Total contribution
1	$1,500	$750	$2,250
2	$1,500	$750	$2,250
3	$1,500	$750	$2,250
4	$1,500	$750	$2,250
5	$1,500	$750	$2,250
6	$1,500	$750	$2,250
7	$1,500	$750	$2,250
8	$1,500	$750	$2,250
9	$1,500	$750	$2,250
10	$1,500	$750	$2,250
Totals:	$15,000	$7,500	$22,500

FIGURE 3

INCLUDES CONTRIBUTIONS ONLY, NO INVESTMENT GROWTH. NOT A GUARANTEE.

> **Baby Boomers**
> Taking advantage of employee stock purchase discounts is important, but it's also important to stay diverse and to reevaluate the amount of company stock you own as you near retirement.

Next, you want to commit to a set amount for your IRA. Depending on whether you have a Traditional, Roth, SIMPLE, or SEP, you have IRS-imposed guidelines on what you can contribute. Ideally, you want to maximize these each year by making some aggressive changes in your budget. If you can't, I advise people to save a minimum of 10 percent of their income, as a general guideline.

Let's take a look at one of my clients to see how big a difference just a little extra savings can make. One of my clients—I'll call him Joe Smith—started setting aside $50 a week in his company 401(k) at age thirty-five. He also set aside $2,500 each year in an IRA, which he then invested in a mutual fund. Now, Joe is sixty-five. Over the past thirty years, he had an average rate of return in the IRA of 4 percent and in the 401(k), a return of 5 percent. He has accumulated a combined total of $305,650 and can withdraw 5 percent each year, giving him $15,282 on top of his Social Security.

Remember, the goal is not necessarily to save enough money to live on for decades in retirement—it's to combine your savings with growth strategies and income plans that help you create an ongoing income stream after you stop working.

Day 8 Checklist

☐ Determine how much it would take to max employer plans.

☐ Consider the impact on your budget and on your risk tolerance (when investing in company stock).

☐ Find ways to reduce your spending so you can contribute to an IRA.

Day 9

Your Preretirement Income Protection

There is no way to plan for your retirement if you don't have an income, which means your current and future income are the most important aspects of your overall retirement savings plan—and that means you need to take steps to protect them.

Your #1 Resource: Disability Insurance

In the United States alone, men and women in their midthirties have a more than 20 percent chance of suffering from a short-term disability each year.[12] A short-term disability could easily result in missing work for weeks, if not months. If you don't have an insurance policy to replace your income during that time, you'll have to dip into your personal savings to pay bills like rent, mortgage, car insurance, and more. If you don't have enough savings, you could end up facing eviction, foreclosure, repossession, and/or bankruptcy.

Millennials

A disability at a young age can be disastrous to your finances—and your retirement planning. According to the Social Security Administration, in 2012 there were more than 2.5 million disabled workers between the ages of 20 and 40, making disability insurance a necessity.

Disability insurance policies will generally take into consideration your current and past earnings as well as your education and experience when deciding what will constitute as a qualifying disability after the "own occupation" period of time ends.

There may be some disabilities that don't require you to miss work entirely, but to reduce your hours each

---

[12]http://www.disabilitycanhappen.org/chances_disability/disability_stats.asp

week. Because of this, you might want to buy a disability policy that promises to also pay a partial benefit.

Another thing to consider when buying disability insurance is the waiting period before benefits begin paying. If you have the savings, you can choose waiting periods from thirty to 360 days where you pay for your own lost wages. A cost-of-living adjustment to raise your benefits in order to keep up with inflation is yet another consideration.

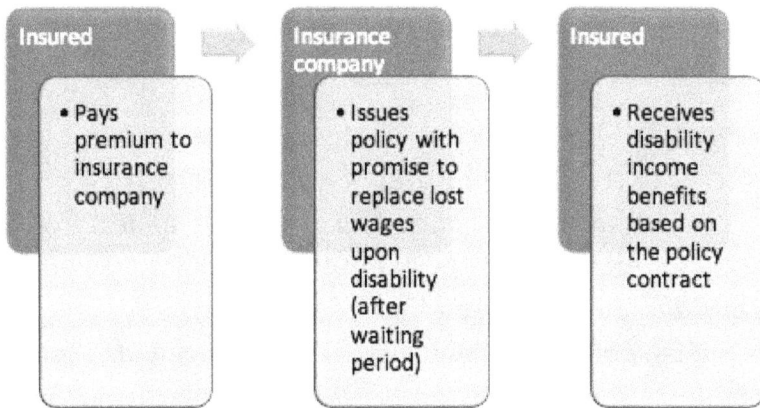

Insured	Insurance company	Insured
• Pays premium to insurance company	• Issues policy with promise to replace lost wages upon disability (after waiting period)	• Receives disability income benefits based on the policy contract

FIGURE 4

HOW DISABILITY INSURANCE POLICIES WORK

Short-Term Disability versus Workers' Compensation

When you're injured at work, you may qualify for workers' compensation insurance to replace your income and pay medical bills. But what happens if you get hurt at home? Or when you go away on the weekend? Or what if the injury is an illness that has nothing to do with your work? This is where a short-term disability policy is vital. They can replace up to six months of income if you are unable to work.

Baby Boomers

Suffering a short-term disability close to your retirement could wreak havoc with your retirement plans. It may force you to take early distributions and pay penalties while also interrupting your ability to keep saving and paying off debt.

Long-Term Disability or Social Security?

Not all disabilities take just weeks or months to heal from. Some last years—maybe even forever. For those, you need to consider long-term disability insurance.

Many people believe that they don't need long-term disability insurance because they can simply qualify for Social Security disability if they have a disability that lasts longer than a year. But there are a few problems with that scenario.

First, with Social Security disability, you have to be unable to perform the duties of ANY job—not just your current job. With a long-term (or even a short-term) disability policy, the qualification terms are much less stringent. Your policy can be designed to begin making payments as soon as you can no longer complete the duties of your own job.

Another issue with Social Security disability is that they'll only approve those with a *permanent* disability. A long-term disability isn't necessarily one that lasts for life. After a long period of therapy and the right medical intervention, it's possible you could recover from certain disabilities. Only a long-term disability will provide payments when you have that chance for recovery.

Finally, it can take years—and multiple appeals—before you are finally approved for Social Security disability. And with no income during that time, you could easily see your savings account emptied. According to the Social Security Administration, roughly 53 percent of claims are denied, which either means lost opportunity for benefits or a lengthy appeals process.[13]

If you want to protect your retirement plan and eventual retirement income, you need to protect your income today, while you're still working.

Work Plans or Personal Plans?

Many employers provide inexpensive short- and long-term disability policies to employees. While these can offer an affordable way to secure coverage, they aren't usually something that you can carry with you when you leave your employer. Additionally, the policies offered may not have as many options for terms and coverage as you actually need. For many people, it's a good idea to talk to an insurance

------

[13] Annual Statistical Report on the Social Security Disability Insurance Program, 2011
https://www.ssa.gov/policy/docs/statcomps/di_asr/2011/sect04.html

agent and see what kind of coverage you can get on your own, outside your employer, before opting into that plan.

Day 9 Checklist

☐ Meet with an agent to discuss disability policy options and premiums.

☐ Consult your budget and savings to determine what kind of waiting period will be affordable.

☐ Find out if you can get an inexpensive disability policy at work.

Day 10

Your Social Security Benefits

Social Security benefits are monthly payments you receive after paying into the Social Security system for a set amount of time and reaching a certain age. These steady, lifelong payments are a great help to many senior citizens, but there are some careful considerations you need to make before you begin taking them.

How Age Factors In

As of the date this text was written, people can choose to trigger Social Security payments beginning at age sixty-two, which is younger than what the Social Security department considers full retirement age.

The 30-Day Retirement Plan

Why does this matter? Because you don't get your full payment amount unless you wait until you've reached your full retirement age—which varies depending on when you were born.[14]

If you choose to take benefits at age sixty-two, you could lose as much as 25 percent of your benefit each month. This can really add up—for example, let's say that Joe Smith is entitled to $1,127 at age sixty-two and $1,624 at age sixty-six, his full retirement age. If he triggers the benefit at age sixty-two and lives for thirty years, he will lose more than $100,000. This can be reversed, however, if you qualify to withdraw your application for benefits and pay back all the benefits you've received. You can only withdraw once per lifetime, however, and you can only do so less than twelve months after you become entitled to receive benefits.

Waiting for full retirement isn't the way to get the highest potential benefit. To do that, you need to wait even longer. If you wait to collect benefits at age seventy, you can gain as much as 8 percent per year from age sixty-six to age seventy.

Choosing Trigger Age

Choosing the age at which to trigger benefits is difficult. For some—those who need the cash desperately—the choice will likely be to take the funds as soon as they become available. But for those who can hold off—either because

---

[14]https://www.ssa.gov/planners/retire/1943.html

they are working longer or because they have savings to tap into—it can obviously be vastly better to wait.

Another consideration, however, is your life expectancy. While few things in life are guaranteed, including life expectancy, you can allow yours to guide the decisions you make about triggering your benefit.

For better or worse, none of us can guarantee the accuracy about our anticipated life expectancy. When considering at what point to trigger Social Security, you want to consider the history of longevity in your family as well as your personal health condition. Generally, it is better to defer as long as possible. When you start taking it at full retirement age, your break-even point ranges between age seventy-seven and age eighty-three—at which time you start taking more out of Social Security than you paid into the system.[15]

Your Postretirement Income Plans

Many people believe that their Social Security benefits are not taxable, but that's not the case. If your provisional income—which is your adjusted gross income, taxable interest, and 50 percent of your Social Security income after retirement from sources such as jobs, pensions, or taxable retirement plan distributions—reaches a high enough level, as much as 85 percent of your Social Security benefits can be taxed. Which means you may want to wait to trigger them until you're certain you'll have a low enough income.

---

[15] http://www.schwab.com/public/schwab/nn/articles/When-Should-You-Take-Social-Security

The Accuracy of Your Benefits

No one is perfect, and that includes the people who work for the Social Security Administration. That's why it's a good idea to set up your account at ssa.gov and check your earnings history for errors.

Who Gets Social Security Benefits?

Social Security benefits are paid out to many individuals for a variety of reasons. Some potential recipients include:

- disabled workers
- divorced spouses and widows/widowers
- children under eighteen who've lost a working parent
- a surviving parent caring for the dependent child of a deceased worker

---

Millennials

Check your Social Security earnings accuracy early and often. It's much easier to fix errors when they are new than when they are decades old.

Your Claiming Strategies

In some cases, you may want to claim spousal benefits rather than your own benefits. When you claim spousal benefits, instead of getting your benefit you'll get 50 percent of the benefit your spouse receives. This is often a good choice for spouses who earned less or stayed home. If you're divorced, you may qualify for spousal benefits from a former spouse, even if you've been remarried.

Social Security Online — Social Security Benefits

www.socialsecurity.gov — Home FAQs Contact Us Search

Office of the Chief Actuary

Effect of Early or Delayed Retirement on Retirement Benefits

Benefit, as a percentage of Primary Insurance Amount (PIA), payable at ages 62-67 and age 70

Year of birth	Normal Retirement Age (NRA)	Credit for each year of delayed retirement after NRA (percent)	Benefit, as a percentage of PIA, beginning at age--						
			62	63	64	65	66	67	70
1924	65	3	80	86 2/3	93 1/3	100	103	106	115
1925-26	65	3 1/2	80	86 2/3	93 1/3	100	103 1/2	107	117 1/2
1927-28	65	4	80	86 2/3	93 1/3	100	104	108	120
1929-30	65	4 1/2	80	86 2/3	93 1/3	100	104 1/2	109	122 1/2
1931-32	65	5	80	86 2/3	93 1/3	100	105	110	125
1933-34	65	5 1/2	80	86 2/3	93 1/3	100	105 1/2	111	127 1/2
1935-36	65	6	80	86 2/3	93 1/3	100	106	112	130
1937	65	6 1/2	80	86 2/3	93 1/3	100	106 1/2	113	132 1/2
1938	65, 2 mo.	6 1/2	79 1/6	85 5/9	92 2/9	98 8/9	105 5/12	111 11/12	131 5/12
1939	65, 4 mo.	7	78 1/3	84 4/9	91 1/9	97 7/9	104 2/3	111 2/3	132 2/3
1940	65, 6 mo.	7	77 1/2	83 1/3	90	96 2/3	103 1/2	110 1/2	131 1/2
1941	65, 8 mo.	7 1/2	76 2/3	82 2/9	88 8/9	95 5/9	102 1/2	110	132 1/2
1942	65, 10 mo.	7 1/2	75 5/6	81 1/9	87 7/9	94 4/9	101 1/4	108 3/4	131 1/4
1943-54	66	8	75	80	86 2/3	93 1/3	100	108	132
1955	66, 2 mo.	8	74 1/6	79 1/6	85 5/9	92 2/9	98 8/9	106 2/3	130 2/3
1956	66, 4 mo.	8	73 1/3	78 1/3	84 4/9	91 1/9	97 7/9	105 1/3	129 1/3
1957	66, 6 mo.	8	72 1/2	77 1/2	83 1/3	90	96 2/3	104	128
1958	66, 8 mo.	8	71 2/3	76 2/3	82 2/9	88 8/9	95 5/9	102 2/3	126 2/3
1959	66, 10 mo.	8	70 5/6	75 5/6	81 1/9	87 7/9	94 4/9	101 1/3	125 1/3
1960 and later	67	8	70	75	80	86 2/3	93 1/3	100	124

Note: Persons born on January 1 of any year should refer to the previous year of birth.

FIGURE 5

THE EFFECT OF EARLY OR DELAYED RETIREMENT

Day 10 Checklist

☐ Visit SSA.gov to check your benefit amounts.

☐ Determine what age your break-even point is.

☐ If you are or were married, find out what your spouse (or former spouse) will get in benefits and determine whether half of that exceeds your personal benefit.

Day 11

Your Estate Plan

While planning for your retirement is the main goal of this book, I don't want to neglect your estate plan. Your estate plan—or legacy plan—is more than just the money you leave behind for your final expenses. It's also about the lasting, ongoing representation you create with your assets—and not just the financial ones.

The estate planning process can be very complex, even for what seems to be a straightforward situation. That's why it's important that everyone consult an attorney and create an estate planning team to protect all angles of their estate and their family's inheritance. Members of an estate planning team can include a financial advisor, insurance advisor, CPA, and trust officer.

Start with the Final Expenses

After you pass away, your family will face a variety of costs, from the cost of your burial or cremation to your service, estate taxes, accounting fees, and carrying costs for various estate holdings such as real estate.

Your first priority is likely to be setting aside final expenses so your family can handle your passing the way you want them to, without creating a financial hardship for them. This can be done without lessening the amount of your estate by having term or permanent life insurance that covers the costs of your final expense plans.

It's also important that you make your final wishes clear. Whether you want a funeral, to be cremated, or want to donate your body and/or organs to science, don't make your family guess at your final wishes.

Move On to the Estate

Next, it's time to plan for the distribution of your financial assets. Many of your accounts, such as your IRAs, 401(k)s, and life insurance policies, will have individual beneficiaries named. Each year, you should check these beneficiaries and make sure you don't need to make any changes. One way you can help reduce the likelihood of changes to your beneficiary designations is to define whether you want the benefits to be *per stirpes* or *per capita*.

Per stirpes is a legal term that designates each branch of the family to receive benefits. When you name beneficiaries per stirpes, and one of the beneficiaries passes away before you, then that individual's branch of the family will receive his or her portion to split equally.

Per capita, on the other hand, separates benefits by generation. That means if you name three beneficiaries and one predeceases you, then the portion of the estate they were to inherit will instead be split equally among the next generation of their surviving relatives.

When it comes to your life insurance policy, if you want to ensure that it avoids potential estate taxation, you may want to name a trust, such as an irrevocable life insurance trust, as beneficiary.

For the remainder of your estate, it's important that you have a will in place. Within the will, you can be as detailed as you want in assigning your assets and property to various individuals, charities, and organizations.

If you want more control over the long-term distribution of your assets, you can consider creating a trust that spells out exactly who gets what, how, and when. You can choose between a revocable trust, in which changes can be made after you've gifted assets, or an irrevocable trust, which is a trust you cannot make changes to after you've gifted assets.

What Your Legacy Means to You

Your legacy is about more than just the financial assets and property you leave behind, but what it means is really up to you. Some ideas for protecting your legacy include:

- Making plans to pass on family heirlooms and historical documents

- Finding ways to continue to honor, after your death, charities, schools, and organizations you care about
- Planning out the succession and continuation of your business
- Making financial plans for future generations

Day 11 Checklist

- [ ] Create an estate planning team.
- [ ] Make sure your final expenses are covered with life insurance.
- [ ] Update your beneficiaries on retirement accounts and life insurance policies.
- [ ] Start thinking about what your legacy means to you.

Day 12

Your Savings Autodrafts

Today you've got a pretty easy day ahead of you. Now that you know how much you're going to set aside each week or month into your various savings accounts, it's time to set up the automatic deposits.

This can be done through your HR department at work, if they allow for autodeposits into multiple accounts. If not, then you can arrange it through your bank, insurance company, or other custodian.

There are some very important reasons that you want to set up all of your savings on autodraft rather than doing it manually. Not only will autodrafts make you more consistent about saving, they will also ensure you don't see the loss of the money from your paycheck. Lastly, this consistent approach to savings contributions helps ensure that you take full advantage of the power of compounding.

Compound interest occurs when the interest paid on your principal sum *also* earns interest—so you're getting paid interest on interest. Year after year. To see how this can add up, take a look at the annual breakdown below and the chart on the next page.

COMPOUNDING INTEREST EXAMPLE

INITIAL INVESTMENT	$1,000.00
ANNUAL INTEREST	1.50%
YEAR	BALANCE
1	$1,015.00
2	$1,030.23
3	$1,045.68
4	$1,061.36
5	$1,077.28
6	$1,093.44
7	$1,109.84
8	$1,126.49
9	$1,143.39
10	$1,160.54
11	$1,177.95
12	$1,195.62
13	$1,213.55
14	$1,231.76
15	$1,250.23
16	$1,268.99
17	$1,288.02
18	$1,307.34
19	$1,326.95
20	$1,346.86
21	$1,367.06
22	$1,387.56
23	$1,408.38
24	$1,429.50
25	$1,450.95

FIGURE 6

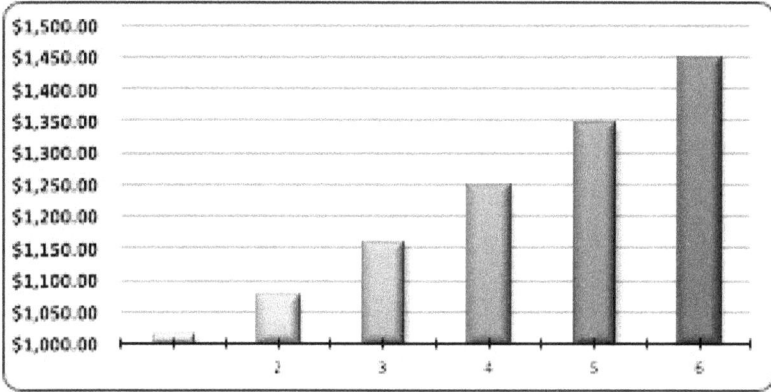

FIGURE 7

Day 12 Checklist

☐ Talk to HR about updating your 401(k) contribution and find out if they can help you set up autodeposits to savings from your paychecks.

☐ If not, set up your own autodeposits from your checking account to your various savings accounts.

Day 13

Your Physical Fitness

You've been working hard to get your retirement plan started, and your head might be swimming with all the new information, so today I'm going to give you an easy(ish) task.

While you've been taxing your mental faculties, you haven't been paying much attention to your physical health, and that's going to change today. Your physical health is the most important asset you have, and it's worth spending some time on preserving it. Not only will this keep you healthier so you can live longer and spend less on healthcare as you age, it will also improve your quality of life by giving you better balance, coordination, and flexibility.

Most doctors will likely recommend a physical fitness routine that includes both aerobic exercise and some strength training. For women, it's important to consider exercises that will strengthen your bones and protect against osteoporosis. Ultimately, you and your doctor must discuss what kind of exercises are best for your current health and physical condition as well as the duration of your workouts and their frequency.

Keeping up with a regular, doctor-approved fitness routine is one of the most important ways to plan for a healthy, happy, *affordable* retirement. Schedule your weekly workouts just as you would any other vital meeting and make them a new way of life—not just a temporary fad.

While some people love being physically fit and are naturally driven toward physical activities, it can take more of an effort for others. Here are a few tips to make both motivating yourself and sticking with it easier.

- Determine the best time of day for working out. Some people have more energy in the morning where others prefer to work out at night. Discover the time of day that works best for you.
- Try different workout locations to determine what is more motivating for you. Some people love taking classes or going to the gym. Others are more comfortable with a home workout and some like to use working out as an excuse to get out of the house and walk around their favorite park.
- Purchase some workout tools for your home. Even if you prefer the gym or outdoor workouts, having a treadmill, Bowflex, free weights, or even just some resistance bands at home means you never have a valid excuse to skip a workout.

- Wear the right shoes, clothes, and equipment. There have been amazing advancements made in workout gear—from sweat-wicking clothes to shoes tailored to your activities to wrist guards to prevent carpal tunnel. Not only can wearing the right workout gear improve your comfort level and performance, it can also help you prevent injuries.
- Keep an exercise log. There's nothing more motivating than grabbing your exercise log and looking back at all the entries, seeing your progress, the changes in your fitness level and endurance, and the stick-to-itiveness that has kept you on track.

From Exercise to Eating Right

Exercise alone isn't enough to keep you healthy—what you fill your body with also plays a giant role. I'm not a medical practitioner, and it's not my place to give nutrition advice, but it's a good idea to talk to your doctor about:

- What supplements will be helpful based on your age, medications, health, and activity level
- What kind of diet is best based on your health, weight, and family history
- Whether you would benefit from calcium, magnesium, and other supplements for bone health
- How to keep your joints healthy
- How much water you need—and whether that should increase as you age

Day 13 Checklist

- [ ] Start researching physical fitness plans that you think you can do.
- [ ] Come up with a plan to improve your nutrition.
- [ ] Talk to your doctor about both your new fitness and nutrition plans before you implement them.

Day 14

Your Spouse

If you're married or you share your life with another person, then the retirement plan you create isn't just about your life after you leave work—it's about your *joint* life. It's about you as a couple and it's also about your significant other as an individual.

There is room in a retirement plan for both partners to have individual goals and dreams as well as joint ones. The key to balancing these is to make sure that you're discussing what those are and that you're compromising so that you both are allowed a sense of fulfillment.

Time to Talk

The only way to make sure you have a realistic, satisfying retirement plan with your spouse or partner is to talk to them about it. You can start this in a fun way, just by exploring your wildest retirement dreams with each other. But as you become more serious about planning, find ways to scale back on these ideal goals until they are both reasonable and satisfying to each of you.

Joint planning isn't just about discussing your ideal lifestyle. It's also about considering each of your bucket lists and finding ways to fit those goals in, when possible.

Retirement planning success for a couple may not be possible without some compromise on both sides. Keep that in mind and try to find innovative ways to be flexible with each other so you both can have a retirement that's close to ideal.

If you aren't sure how to get started in this conversation, use the following list of questions to start exploring the topic with each other:

- At what age do each of you want to retire? Is there a big gap between your answers? How can you make that work? Does the spouse who wants to retire early have a plan for spending that time alone? Will the working spouse resent the retired spouse? How will this impact your Social Security payments (see Day 10 for more information)? How will the nonworking spouse handle medical insurance?
- What do you envision an average day being like in retirement? Does one spouse see him- or herself constantly on the go while the other envisions days spent rocking on the porch? Can you both be

satisfied living independently so the other can enjoy their ideal?

- Where do you want to live in retirement? Do you both want to stay put, or do you want to make a drastic change?
- What kinds of luxuries are important for you to maintain during retirement? Do you both want to enjoy dinners out and frequent travel? Or is a frugal lifestyle with library books and thrift-store shopping satisfying for both of you?

Define Responsibilities

Each partner should have some responsibility when it comes to retirement planning and the financial prep that goes along with it. If both individuals work, then they should each be saving money toward retirement. It's important to discuss what each of your financial savings responsibilities will be and to talk about the most advantageous way to accomplish this, whether that's with 401(k) contributions or IRAs, or both.

A spouse or partner with no income also has responsibilities. They must help make sure that the couple's spending doesn't exceed the budget, so they can continue to save money toward their joint dream. They can also help hold the working spouse accountable for saving money.

In addition, once you determine how much you need to start saving to get to your joint retirement goals, you have to look at your current spending and budget and make adjustments that allow you to save. This is, again, something you both need to discuss, compromise on, and agree on. If you aren't both committed to it, it simply won't work.

Schedule Periodic Reviews

People change. Minds change. Priorities change. This propensity for change is just one of the reasons you and your spouse or partner need to periodically review your retirement goals and objectives. But it's not the only reason. Changes in tax codes, inflation rates, housing costs, and more can all impact the success and viability of your plan.

When you're thirty or forty years out from retirement, an annual discussion to make sure your savings is on track is probably sufficient. As you get within ten years or less from retirement, more frequent discussions of both savings progress and lifestyle priorities are important.

Day 14 Checklist

☐ Write a list of things you need to discuss with your spouse or partner.

☐ Choose a date and time to talk to them. Make sure the date and time are convenient for them and that they understand what's on the agenda.

Day 15

Your Postretirement Income Needs

One of your ultimate goals is to find a way to transform your retirement savings into a steady stream of income once you've retired. But at some point, you have to have some idea of how much income is enough.

Considerations in Postretirement Income Needs

Generally speaking, most people require 60 to 80 percent of their preretirement income each year in retirement. This may strike you as odd, since expenses are generally less once you leave the working world, your kids move out, and you downsize into retirement, but there are many threats to your savings and expenses that account for this increase need, including:

- Inflation: Inflation is the rise of prices for goods and services that we can generally expect to experience each year. Social Security usually adjusts for inflation through a cost-of-living adjustment (COLA) although sometimes, like in 2016, they decide that reduced prices on some goods (in 2016, it was a reduction in the price of gas) makes enough of a difference to retirees to result in a lowered, or lack of, COLA.
- Tax increases: Taxes on purchases can increase as sales taxes rise. Taxes on income can increase as income taxes rise. In addition, seniors can face increases in property taxes, taxes on services such as cable, and so on.

But that's not all. Retirees also need to find ways to protect their potential income from something called sequence of returns risk. You already know that your earnings or returns on various investments fluctuate based on many factors, including market performance and interest rates. This fluctuation means that sometimes there will be poor performance/low returns at a time when you need to liquidate and free up some cash. When you do this early on in your retirement, it means that you are more likely to run out of savings later on than if you encountered those same poor returns later in your retirement. This is sequence of returns risk.

The next consideration is in your lifestyle expenses, which will be covered in more detail on Day 24 when we look at your three postretirement budgets.

Day 15 Checklist

☐ Write down what 60, 70, and 80 percent of your current income is. Keep these numbers handy so you can see them again when you work on your postretirement budgets on Day 24.

Day 16

Your Bucket List

"Kicking the bucket" is a popular phrase often used to make it easier to deal with the concept of death. It's from this popular euphemism that we get the term *bucket list*, which describes a list of experiences that a person would like to have, or things they'd like to accomplish, before they pass away.

There are some experiences and achievements that are so meaningful to each of us, we want to ensure that we can accomplish them within our lifetimes. Whether that's running with the bulls in Pamplona, flying in a helicopter over the spectacular scenery of Oahu, or getting on stage to perform in some way, these lifetime aspirations are the items that belong on your bucket list.

Some people are lucky enough to be able to complete their various bucket list items throughout their lives. Others find that they have many—if not all of them—still to do during their retirement. If you're not careful, that can become a very expensive objective and, if you're on a budget, maybe even impossible.

That's why it's important to create a strategy around creating your bucket list and organizing your postretirement cash flow so you can complete it.

Millennials

You may be working now on fulfilling the wishes that might be on another person's bucket list. This is great—but just make sure it's not hurting your ability to save for the future.

Working Your Bucket List Around Your Budget

The point of a bucket list is twofold. First, it helps ensure that you can really focus on creating your most ideal, meaningful life. Second, it helps you organize the expense of your must-do items. For example, let's say that you've always wanted to take a trip to Greece. This is where your family is originally from, and it's extremely important to you to get there someday. When you have this on your bucket list, you can prioritize it over trips to other areas that don't mean as much to you. You can also make a budget for it and set aside funds from your retirement income to pay for this trip. By creating this budget, you can then see what's realistic about your plans—maybe switch that five-star, waterfront hotel to a less expensive hostel in town.

When considering your bucket list AND your budget, remember the following:

- Not all bucket list items need to cost money. While some of the things you want to experience and accomplish may require some capital, you should also list those free, personal accomplishments you want to achieve, such as learning another language using online tools or practicing to make that hole-in-one shot in your backyard.

- Bucket lists should consist solely of experiences you are driven to do during your life. It shouldn't contain one-off things you think would be fun, but meaningful things you *really* have a drive to accomplish.

- Because of the meaningfulness and importance of bucket list items, you can't expect to knock them off month after month. Make your list knowing that you're going to take your time and really enjoy each experience and accomplishment.

- Give yourself options in terms of the cost of each bucket list item. Using my earlier example—the trip to Greece—write down some ways that you can take the trip and be completely satisfied but not have it cost your entire life's savings.

Day 16 Checklist

☐ Write your bucket list!

Day 17

Your Personal Savings Account

If you're reading this book, then accumulating retirement savings is probably one of your top priorities. To actually get adequate retirement savings, however, it's critical that you not ignore your personal (nonretirement) savings.

I believe that people should have three types of savings—I call them yellow, green, and red buckets. The money saved in your yellow bucket is your liquid cash for emergencies and short-term needs.[16] This will generally be in a low-interest, very liquid account such as a money

---

[16]David Vick, *Bat-Socks, Vegas & Conservative Investing*

market or savings. In general, this should account for at least 10 percent of your entire cash-asset base.

Next, you have your green bucket, which is the money that's going to pay out your retirement income. I refer to this bucket as your *mailbox money*, or lifetime guaranteed income. Employers aren't providing employees with pensions anymore, which means that each of us has to put money aside in our green bucket and look for investments such as annuities that provide guaranteed income throughout our retirement.

The final bucket, the red one, is for savings that you are comfortable getting into a little risk with—which means it's often not needed in the short-term and is invested in stocks, bonds, and mutual funds.

With personal savings, you can gradually accrue the funds for large purchases, such as vacations and house down payments, ultimately helping minimize debt. Personal savings also gives you the power to create a source of emergency funds. With the emergency cash in your yellow bucket, you have the opportunity to truly control your financial situation and avoid debt, which will lead to increased consistency and success in retirement saving.

The Bucket Approach to Personal Savings

Personal savings doesn't have to be complicated. It can even be as simple as just putting as much as you can, each month, into a taxable savings account opened with your bank. That's it—that's all it takes to increase your financial control and odds of retirement saving success.

For some people, however, a more defined approach works better. If you think you would benefit from this, consider having multiple savings accounts for various categories. For example, you might set up one savings account for vacation savings, one for holiday spending, one for future big-ticket purchases, and one for emergencies. Depending on your risk level, timeline for use, and liquidity needs, you can decide whether to put the funds for various buckets in a money market account, which generally offers more aggressive savings rates than savings accounts; in a CD, which can impose early withdrawal penalties; in a checking account for frequent withdrawals; or even in mutual funds, where the funds may be exposed to various market risks.

If you don't want the hassle of multiple accounts, you can simply set up a spreadsheet or use a finance app to track your savings deposits and allocate them to various savings categories. Apps such as Mint or Qapital can provide innovative ways to track and categorize your savings.

Day 17 Checklist

☐ Look into options for interest-bearing savings or money market accounts that give immediate access to funds.

☐ Determine how much of your personal savings contributions should be attributed to each type of savings account.

☐ Open additional accounts for your mid- and long-term savings—or choose an app to organize your contributions into the appropriate buckets.

Day 18

Your Retirement Lifestyle Goals

While travel, bucket list fulfillment, and enjoying new hobbies are all aspects of your retirement, they are more like highlights of your life, not the routine. Your everyday activities—paying bills, doing housework, going to the doctor, watching television, visiting friends, and so on, make up the bulk of your time and they are what define your ultimate retirement lifestyle.

Lifestyle Decisions

Heading into retirement, it's important to have a well-defined idea of the kind of lifestyle you want. The word "lifestyle" can mean many things to many people, so let me lay out a few factors that are involved:

- Where you will live (what town, city, country, state)
- What kind of home you will have (house, cottage, apartment, condo, duplex)
- What your average monthly budget will be (including insurance premiums, groceries, utilities, etc.)
- What kind of car you'll drive
- What kind of luxuries you'll allow yourself (cable, hired help, frequent dinners out, lots of shopping, etc.)
- Your various income sources and amounts (pension, 401(k)s, IRAs, Social Security, beneficiary IRAs, guaranteed income, inheritance). While considering the potential of each of these sources is vital, it's also important not to count on them reaching certain levels. For example, the inheritance you think you're going to get may not be what you actually receive. You can only count on those sources and investments that are guaranteed.

Within all of that, you have to make sure your monthly spending is low enough to also afford:

- fun travel
- travel to visit family
- bucket list fulfillment

- hobby spending (new golf clubs, ceramics classes, weekly bingo attendance, etc.)

But we're not done yet. You also need to make sure your lifestyle allows you to afford:

- emergency expenses (home repairs, car breakdowns, medical treatment, etc.)
- future long-term care needs
- a potentially long retirement
- inflation and taxes
- home, car, and personal physical maintenance
- the legacy you want to leave behind

Millennials

With so many decades ahead of you before retirement, evaluating your *current* lifestyle is also a good idea. The more extravagantly you spend now, the less money you have to save for later.

Lifestyle Intangibles

Not all of your lifestyle planning needs revolve around money and other tangibles. It's also critical to think about the way you want to spend your TIME. A happy and fulfilling retirement isn't just about having enough money to last, it's also about satisfying your need to learn, create, work, laugh, play, and so on.

It's important to clearly define this aspect of your lifestyle along with the financial because they are often intertwined. For example, let's say you realize that your lifestyle would be much cheaper in another state, yet your intangible lifestyle needs involve spending lots of time with your friends—who do not live in this other state. As such, you need to adjust your planning so that you can remain near your friends while still reducing your overall lifestyle costs.

Day 18 Checklist

☐ Write down the various lifestyle preferences you have for your retirement years.

Day 19

Your Physical

Your money, cars, homes, and collectibles aren't the only valuable assets you bring into retirement with you. Your health is the one asset that ensures you can enjoy all the others—and it's also the asset that can be hardest to recover.

I'm not a doctor, so I'm not going to go into a lot of detail here, but what I'm asking you to do today is to schedule an appointment for a physical.

Caring for an Aging Body

No matter how old you are right now, your body is aging. Tomorrow it will be older than it is today, and today it is older than it was last year. As you age, even if you think you feel about the same as you did when you were twenty, health issues can be creeping up on you—and you need to be aware of them to treat them and make sure they don't get out of control. Some of the biggest problems facing men and women as they age are:

- High blood pressure: Also called hypertension, high blood pressure means the heart must work harder to pump blood through your body. While genetics is a big cause of hypertension, it can also be caused by weight gain, smoking, insufficient exercise, and even stress.
- High cholesterol: Cholesterol is a type of fat that is found in your blood. Some cholesterol (LDL) builds up and can create blockages in your arteries. This can be caused by genetics, obesity, lack of exercise, and even smoking.
- Type 2 diabetes: The most common form of diabetes, type 2 occurs when your body becomes resistant to insulin. This can be caused by age, a high-carb or high-fat diet, obesity, and lack of exercise.

Taking Care of Eyes and Teeth

Your GP isn't the only doctor you need to see regularly. You also need to see your dentist and your ophthalmologist regularly.

Not only will regular dental appointments help you keep your teeth far into retirement, it will also help reduce your likelihood of getting gum disease, and that means it may reduce your risk factors for heart disease, since the two have been found to be connected.

Speaking of heart disease, your ophthalmologist can help you with early detection since eye exams can reveal problems with arteries that may be caused by blood clots and other blockages.

Health Is Dynamic: Go Back Regularly

No matter how great your blood test results are at your next physical, you still need to make sure you're going back at least annually to keep an eye on your ongoing health.

Prevention is crucial to living a long life, and early detection is key to preventing many diseases from spreading. Take care of your body the way you take care of your money!

Day 19 Checklist

☐ Call your GP and schedule a physical.
☐ Call your dentist and ophthalmologist and schedule appointments.
☐ Create a reminder to go back to the doctor as often as recommended.

Day 20

Your Family

After you and your spouse or partner have spoken about your overall retirement plans and timelines, it's important to talk to the rest of your family—namely, your kids.

Why Talk to Your Kids

Retirement isn't just about you and your spouse/partner—it's about your whole family. Your kids want to know that you have a plan in place to comfortably and safely support yourself. They want to know that you're saving money and that you'll have insurance to cover things such as long-term care expenses.

Not only does this help your family feel confident that you will be well cared for during your retirement but it also helps relieve some of the stress they may feel as they face the realities of your aging.

You see, according to NPR, as many as eleven million adults need assistance in their activities of daily living (ADLs).[17] That means help with things like dressing, bathing, and eating. If you haven't got a plan for long-term care insurance (which is covered in more detail on Day 27), then your kids may have to fill in the gaps and care for you or pay to ensure that you have the care you need. By discussing your plans with them, they know what to expect and can give their input on what they see themselves capable of helping with (both financially and physically) in the future.

Gen X

For those of you with millennial children, your discussion time can be a great opportunity to teach your kids about what you wish you'd done differently at their age to prepare for retirement.

Millennials

Don't be afraid to ask your parents about their retirement plans if they don't bring them up to you!

---

[17]http://www.npr.org/2012/05/08/151970188/long-term-care-insurance-who-needs-it

> **Baby Boomers**
> Use your family discussion as an opportunity to talk to your gen X and millennial children about their retirement plans. Doing so can ensure they're planning the way they should be.

Checklist for Discussion

- If you're relocating, discuss how often you can travel to see them and how often you'd open your home to them.
- Make clear your preferences regarding long-term care and living arrangements when you can no longer live independently.
- Tell them about your power of attorney choices (discussed in more detail on Day 28).

Day 20 Checklist

☐ Write a list of things you need to discuss with your family.

☐ Choose a date and time to talk to them. Make sure the date and time are convenient for them and that they understand what's on the agenda.

Day 21

Your Health Screening

By now, you've done a lot of planning—maybe more than you've ever done, and all pretty much without breaking a sweat. Congratulations!

After completing your bucket list, talking to your spouse or partner, and discussing your plans with your family, you also realize just how much you have to look forward to.

But you probably want to do more than just look forward to retirement—you actually want to get there and stay there as long as possible with as few health problems as you can manage. And that means you need to keep up with your health screenings for diseases like prostate cancer, breast cancer, and colon cancer.

What to Screen and When

You might remember that on Day 3 I talked about going to the doctor regularly. In addition to the regular physical you schedule with your GP to look at your blood pressure, cholesterol, weight, and all those other numbers, you need to consider the annual screenings that are important based on your gender and age. Women of all ages should be getting regular well-woman exams. The medical community has many conflicting viewpoints over when men and women should think about colonoscopies and when women need to think about mammograms and men need to think about prostate exams. Talk to your doctor to see what age they recommend beginning these exams.

Gen X

Many of you are just now reaching the age at which you need to get serious about annual screenings. It's important that you make this mental adjustment and get them done!

The Importance of Early Detection

Let's look at a few facts to really communicate the importance of early screening:

- Studies have shown that getting 80 percent of people to take part in health screenings could reduce colon cancer deaths by as many as 200,000 within twenty years.[18]

- Cervical cancer deaths have declined by 70 percent since 1950 thanks to women having Pap smears.[8]
- Five-year survival rates for men with prostate cancer are 100 percent when it's detected early.[19]

Not only can health screenings help prevent death but thanks to early detection, more people can expect to reach full recovery with less aggressive treatment methods, meaning fewer side effects and less expense for treatment.

Day 21 Checklist

☐ Talk to your GP about when you should start your health screenings.
☐ Make appointments now for those that you need to start doing annually.

---

[18]https://www.cancer.org/latest-news/impact-of-achieving-80-by-2018-screening-goal.html

[19]http://www.canaryfoundation.org/wp-content/uploads/EarlyDetectionFactSheet.pdf

Day 22

Your Postretirement Income Plan

When you retire, you probably don't want to look at your dwindling savings balance and try to imagine that supporting you for an unknown number of years. Instead, you probably want to think about your savings in terms of the income it can bring in.

There are many different products you can choose to create income from savings, some of which have built-in lifetime guarantees. Let's take a look at some of the many income-producing products out there to choose from.

Dividend Stocks

While all dividend stocks (those equity positions that pay out a portion of profits to shareholders in the form of dividends) can provide income to retirees, preferred stocks might be the most sensible choice. Common stocks that pay dividends usually pay less than preferred stocks and they also don't have priority claim on dividends should a company become insolvent.

Either way, it's important to remember that dividends are only paid when the company has profit and votes to pay them—which means they aren't always guaranteed, and that can be difficult to deal with when relying on them for income.

Bonds and CDs

The coupon, or interest payment, paid on bonds and CDs can create a helpful income stream for retirees. Before choosing bonds and CDs, however, retirees need to think about the amount of money they are paying in principal and the maturity dates of the bonds and CDs they choose. You see, when you need to get at that principal before maturity, possibly because of a large, unexpected, or emergency expense, you could be charged a penalty for early withdrawal. If you have all your savings tied into a bond or CD with a far-out maturity date, this is going to really restrict your access to funds for unexpected expenses.

Another concern of bond and CD investors is something called interest rate risk. Because interest rates are constantly changing, it's possible that when your CDs and bonds mature, you will have trouble finding a new bond or CD that pays as high a rate of interest. This will have a tremendous impact on the income you can expect.

One way to help minimize these risks is to create bond and CD ladders. These are strategies that involve staggering the maturity dates of multiple bond and CD purchases so that you often have them maturing and, thus, principal coming available for use or for re-investment.

Annuities

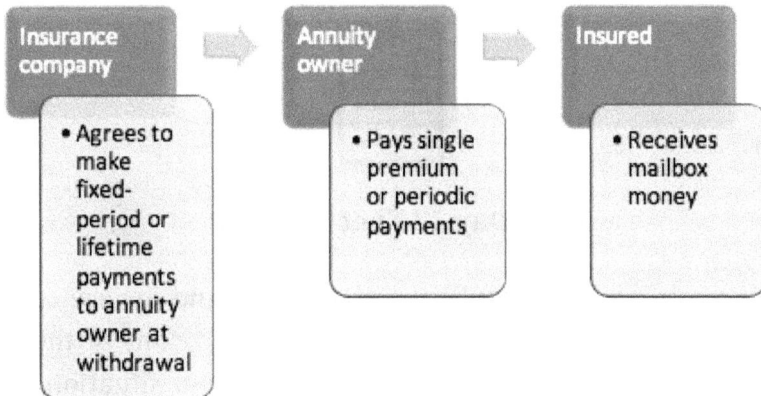

FIGURE 8

HOW ANNUITIES WORK

One solution that helps many retirees enjoy what I like to call "mailbox money"—a regular check for income every month for life—is an annuity.

An annuity is a contract issued by a life insurance company. With the proper design, an annuity can be set up with a rider, called a guaranteed minimum income benefit (GMIB), that guarantees a stable income for life—no matter how long you live. The amount of the income varies depending on when you trigger it, the total amount of your investment, and features of the rider. With the right annuity, performance the rider can be excluded from the influence of a falling market.

Annuities have a lot of flexibility in design options, allowing you to add benefits discussed in other chapters, such as long-term care coverage and death benefits.

Day 22 Checklist

☐ Talk to a few financial advisors and insurance agents to determine the pros and cons of the various income investments for your situation.

Day 23

Your Debt

No one wants to bring debt into retirement with them, but your debt isn't going to disappear on its own. You have to come up with a plan to pay it off. Thankfully, there are many methods of debt eradication that you can consider.

Debt Consolidation

Going through the right debt consolidation company can mean reducing the overall interest paid on your debt, reducing your payments, paying debt earlier, and even making monthly payments easier. But you have to be careful when going this route, because you need to truly understand what the company is offering you. While some offer a loan that pays off your existing debts and you repay the loan, others don't offer credit counseling or settlement.

If this seems like an option you want to explore, make sure you talk to several companies and compare their services and costs so that you can find the best fit.

Personal Debt Repayment Schedule

It's not necessary to go through a credit counseling or debt consolidation company. If you're disciplined and committed, you can come up with your own personal debt repayment schedule that's more aggressive than the minimum payment schedule set up by your various creditors.

When you develop your own schedule, there are a couple of methods you can choose, depending on which will be the most motivating to you.

1. Smallest to largest: Some people like to focus on aggressively paying off their smallest debts first and then, as those are paid off, rolling the payments they once made on those paid-off debts over into the next smallest debt, and so on. While this might not be the most cost-effective method, seeing small balances getting paid off can be very motivating.

2. High interest first: If you want to focus on reducing your overall interest payments as much as possible, then you want to attack your highest interest debts first. Look at your wasteful liabilities—such as credit cards, personal loans, and other debt that offers no equity or potential return—and pay off those with the highest interest rates first. There are many online calculators you can use to help you determine which debt is most expensive to hold.

Out with the Old—Restricting the New

Getting out of debt is amazing, but it's just a start. In order to ensure you're not bringing debt into retirement, you also need a plan for avoiding new debt after you've paid off the existing debt. One of the best ways to keep yourself out of debt once you pay it all off is to keep yourself on a budget, something covered on Day 7. A budget helps you restrict your spending to less than your earnings so you never have to rely on credit to get you through between paychecks.

Budgeting also helps you with saving money—and saving money is absolutely vital in avoiding debt. With savings, you can dip into your personal funds to pay for emergencies, vacations, and to buy big-ticket items—even cars.

Life insurance may be another option for debt avoidance, as a properly designed policy can give you the power to borrow money from yourself. This is discussed in more detail on Day 6.

Baby Boomers

As the generation closest to retirement, it's critical that you stay out of debt once you pay it off. With fewer working years to earn income, you have less chance of paying new debt off than other generations.

Watching Your Credit

One of the reasons controlling your debt is important is because too much debt, or too many late payments, can have an adverse effect on your personal credit rating. That means other loans, such as auto loans or mortgages, will have higher interest rates, thereby increasing your overall expenses and reducing the amount of money you can put toward savings.

Checking your credit report every year is an important part of managing your overall financial health. To do this, you can contact each of the three credit reporting agencies—TransUnion, Experian, and Equifax—and double-check all the information they have. You need to look at:

- the personal data they've collected
- the list of creditors, balances, and payment histories
- the new inquiries run on your credit report

Information that is old or just plain wrong needs to be reported so it can be corrected or removed. Both inquiries being made and your various creditors can clue you in on any issues you may have with identity theft.

In addition to allowing you to dispute incorrect items and catch instances of identity theft, running your credit report can give you an idea of what you need to do to improve your overall credit rating.

Day 23 Checklist

- [ ] Take out all your statements and determine what your debt is.
- [ ] Prioritize your debt and use your budget to set up payments based on that prioritization.
- [ ] Make sure you're paying more than minimums as often as possible.
- [ ] Find ways to avoid taking on new debt.
- [ ] Request your credit report from all three credit reporting agencies and check for inaccuracies and suspicious activity. Then come up with a plan to help improve your credit rating.

Day 24

Your Three Postretirement Budgets

During both your working years and your retirement, a budget creates a guideline for your spending that ensures you don't spend more than you can afford. It holds you accountable and provides a path that helps ensure you won't run out of money after you stop collecting a paycheck.

Spending some time now, while you're still working, to create the budget you plan to use during retirement is also a way to guide your current savings. When you have a clear picture of what you'll need to meet your lifestyle expectations after retirement and what you need to cover healthcare, Medicare, Advantage plans, etc., then you have a helpful guide for what you still need to save before retirement.

But creating one postretirement budget isn't really good enough—I think you should create three.

Why Three Postretirement Budgets?

The lifestyle you'll live in retirement isn't etched in stone just because you create a budget for it. You have no idea what will happen once you actually retire—what global and economic events will impact your spending, what you will and won't enjoy doing with your time, what opportunities for travel, relocation and adventure might come up. By creating three different budgets, you have a means of designing several postretirement lifestyle potential scenarios with a variety of living expenses and incomes that you can shift to throughout retirement, depending on your actual financial situation.

> **Millennials**
> This may seem like an odd exercise when retirement is so far off, but it can be a really good wake-up call that helps you understand just how aggressively you'll need to save in order to get where you want to be in retirement.

Budget One: The Ideal

The first postretirement budget you design will probably be your ideal one. This is the budget that assumes all your savings is doled out as steady income, all prices for groceries, gas, and other supplies stays the same, your tax rate is reasonable, and your living expenses are easy to handle. This budget might include your ideal travel schedule, hobbies, lots of dinners out, and social events. Keep in mind, however, that *ideal* doesn't mean *fantasy*—this isn't a budget created for someone with unlimited income.

Budget Two: The Lesser

The second budget is where you start getting more conservative. You can estimate your expenses and taxes higher, you can anticipate some negative impact on your income, and you can reduce your discretionary spending as needed.

Budget Three: Financial Crisis

In the third budget, you want to think in terms of a financial crisis. For this budget, you want to take aggressive steps to reduce expenses including relocation, downsizing, and cutting out discretionary spending on travel, hobbies, and social events so that you can respond to a sudden health crisis, loss of job and early retirement, loss of money from investments, or other adverse financial situation.

Three Phases of Retirement

According to the Commission for Financial Capability, there are three phases of life that each retiree goes through:

- Active: This is the time early in retirement when you're aggressively pursuing life and all the hobbies and enjoyments you had to put on hold while you worked and raised a family.

- Passive: This is when you've slowed down, accepted a calmer retirement routine, and aren't traveling as much.
- Supported: This is the phase when you may be getting in-home help or living in a home with assistance.

While the initial three postretirement budgets you make will likely have the active phase in mind, it's a good idea to create some budgets for your passive and supported phases as well.

Day 24 Checklist

☐ Create your three postretirement budgets.

Day 25

Your Future Living Arrangements

There are many decisions to make as you head into retirement, but one of the most important is where you will live. Not only can your home's type and location dictate your monthly expenses, it can also have a huge influence on your overall happiness, comfort, health, and social life.

Defining Your Wants and Needs

When it comes to choosing where to live, you have to consider two things: your wants and your needs. While your wants are flexible, your needs are not. Some of the needs you have to think about include:

- physical restrictions you face or anticipate in the future
- postretirement budget and income
- cost of the home, maintenance, and insurance
- cost of living—groceries, utilities, travel, etc.
- whether it can accommodate your local travel needs (public transportation, walking distance, etc.)

Some of the wants include:
- type of climate (this can fall under a need, depending on your health)
- size of your home
- proximity to children, family, and friends
- nearness to chosen activities and services (library, senior center, etc.)

Downsizing and Relocating Considerations

Seniors often choose to downsize their homes after retirement, since their kids are grown and living on their own. Downsizing can have a lot of benefits and should definitely be considered as it can allow you to:

- realize financial gains upon sale of the house
- reduce overall expenses, including property taxes, maintenance, and utilities
- free you up to move to a more convenient location

Another step often taken by retirees is to emigrate from the United States to a less expensive country. Doing so can help save you money both in lowered living expenses and—in some cases—lower taxes. It can offer you a type of lifestyle, attitude, and climate you can't enjoy in the United States and can offer you access to cheap, cutting-edge healthcare.

But expatriation isn't just a walk in the park. Many of the cheapest countries to move to lack the same infrastructure as the United States. You may have to learn a new language to communicate effectively and may not have access to the same social and government programs as you do in the US. Political and social instability in many third-world countries can also make them dangerous places for everyone—especially seniors. You may have trouble adapting to the food and culture, you may not have access to safe drinking water, and you may even lack access to decent healthcare.

> ### Millennials
> With the massive power of compounding on your side, living an affordable lifestyle NOW—while you're young—is a great way to ensure you have plenty of money saved for retirement.

Reverse Mortgage

For some seniors, a reverse mortgage offers additional options in retirement that mean they can stay in their home and avoid relocation altogether. A reverse mortgage is an agreement wherein a lender agrees to make payments over time to the senior in exchange for the equity in the house after the senior passes away. Mortgage payments back to the lender don't need to be made during the borrower's lifetime. Instead, the balance is paid back at death either out of the estate or out of funds from the sale of the property.

To qualify for a reverse mortgage, there must not be any outstanding loans on the home. Once the loan goes through, the homeowner must continue to pay property taxes and insurance.

In order to maximize the benefits of a reverse mortgage, seniors might consider putting the funds into an annuity with a guaranteed income payment. That way they can turn their loan into mailbox money that they can rely on.

A reverse mortgage is a potentially dangerous option for seniors; it can impact their legacy, involve excessive fees, and impact eligibility for certain social programs. As such, it's important that you consult an advisor before taking this step.

Day 25 Checklist

☐ Think about how it might benefit you to move, downsize, or relocate.

☐ Consider the personal and emotional drawbacks of each (including how it could affect your family relationships).

Day 26

Your Current Savings Plan

If you've been doing the exercises in the order laid out in the book then right now, on Day 26, you're in a good place. You've seen, or are scheduled to see, your doctor. You're taking control of your health and starting to exercise. You've got your retirement accounts open and contributions heading into them. You've spoken to your spouse/partner and family to clarify your postretirement goals. Even if you haven't yet done any of these things, and you've decided to kick off your journey at Day 26, it's time to ask yourself a difficult question:

Are you saving enough?

This is a hard question to answer and may not even have a single, right response. Right now, you're saving for many things—your future retirement and for the money you may need over the next few years for vacations, homes, cars, emergencies, and big-ticket purchases. That's a lot to have on your plate, and you need to find a way to compartmentalize each of these savings priorities and measure your needs.

Focusing on Retirement First

In general, you should expect to need 60 to 80 percent of your current income every year that you are retired. Look at your anticipated retirement age, your anticipated Social Security benefit, and your life expectancy. If you multiply your current income by .65, divide that by twelve, then subtract your monthly Social Security benefit, you are looking at a rough estimate of your monthly income needs after retirement. Will that amount work to meet the income needs outlined on the three postretirement budgets (found on Day 24)?

Next, you need to multiply that monthly number by twelve to get your annual income needs. Then, you need to factor in the age at which you plan to retire, the number of years you can reasonably expect to be retired, and a safe rate of return—say around 3 percent or so.

One easier way to determine whether you're saving enough for retirement is to look at income-generating products with lifetime guarantees, such as annuities, and determine how much you need to put into the annuity to generate the income you need—for life.

Saving for Now

In addition to saving for retirement, you also need to save for your more immediate future. Some of the things you need to consider include:

- Saving for deductibles: If you have insurance policies with deductibles (i.e., auto, home, health), you need to make sure you have enough set aside to pay them—sometimes multiple times per year—when disaster strikes.
- Saving for emergencies: Generally, you want to make sure you have six months of income saved so that you can deal with a layoff, job loss, or other emergency.
- Big-ticket purchases: The more you save, the less debt you will carry when you face expenses such as buying a home, buying a car, making home repairs, or replacing an old or damaged appliance. Look at your short-, mid-, and long-term purchasing goals to help determine whether you are saving enough to help make all of these purchases.

Day 26 Checklist

☐ Review your current savings contributions. Measure whether you're saving enough for:
- emergencies
- deductibles
- big-ticket purchases
- short-, mid-, and long-term goals

☐ Reevaluate your budget if you find you're coming up short on any of these categories.

Day 27

Your Long-Term Care Insurance

Today, your goal is to start researching your options for long-term care insurance. It's an unfortunate truth, but it's one we all need to face: you will not always be as healthy as you are today. In fact, according to the American Association for Long-Term Care Insurance, in 2009 more than 40 percent of people over age sixty-five reported having limitations in their ability to complete daily functions, with 18 percent reporting difficulty with at least one *activity of daily living.*[20]

---

[20]http://www.aaltci.org/long-term-care-insurance/learning-center/long-term-care-statistics.php

Let's talk about what that means in layman's terms. Activities of daily living, also referred to as ADLs, are the common, everyday tasks you do to maintain a normal, healthy life. They include activities such as:

- bathing
- feeding yourself
- dressing
- cleaning
- self-grooming
- toileting
- transferring from walking to sitting and getting back up again

Because ADLs deal with functional activities, rather than medical activities, any assistance you need to complete them is not considered "medical" assistance and is, therefore, not covered by Medicare. That means you need to have some kind of long-term care plan in place to protect you should you become one of the 40 percent of those over age sixty-five who needs help with one or more of these activities.

Long-Term Care Insurance Policies

A long-term care insurance policy is a specifically designed insurance contract to help pay for the costs associated with nonmedical care, either at home or in a nursing facility. Benefits of a policy might include:

- adult daycare services
- physical therapy

- home health aide services
- respite care for caregivers

The cost of a policy depends on many factors, including:

- The age of the policy holder: The older you are, the more likely you'll need to use the policy, so the more expensive it becomes. Additionally, you may have premium increases along the way.
- The daily benefit limit: Each policy allows the policyholder to choose a daily benefit limit that determines the daily maximum costs the policy will cover. The lower your limit, the less expensive the policy will be.
- The waiting/elimination period: Policies allow policyholders to choose a length of time during which they will cover their own long-term care expenses and the policy won't. This is called the elimination period. The shorter the elimination period, the sooner the policy will have to start paying, and the more expensive the premium will be. You can generally expect a standard waiting period to be between ninety and one hundred days.
- Duration limits: Policies can have a limit to the length of time they will cover the long-term care needs of the policyholder. For example, some policies may offer lifetime coverage while others may only cover LTC needs for up to five years. The longer your policy's duration, the more expensive the premium.

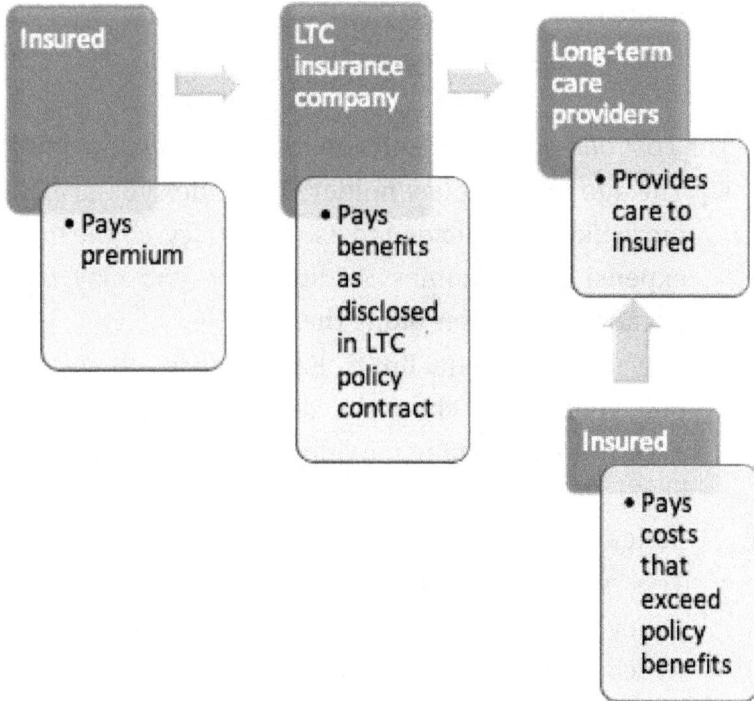

FIGURE 9

HOW LONG-TERM CARE POLICIES WORK

Alternative Options for Long-Term Care Coverage

Due to the expense and complexity of long-term care policies, many people instead turn to alternative coverage options, such as hybrid annuities, hybrid life policies, and life insurance riders, all of which can provide some long-term care benefits.

One of the benefits of hybrid annuities and life policies is that funds that are not used for long-term care expenses are instead used to fulfill other contractual promises, such as income and death benefit. That means that instead of paying for a LTC policy that they never use, the insured pays for a benefit that is transferred to another aspect of the policy.

Day 27 Checklist

☐ Talk to an agent about the benefits of an annuity or life insurance policy versus a long-term care insurance policy.

☐ Compare prices for various types of coverage before deciding how to proceed.

Day 28

Your Power of Attorney

You may not always be in the right state of mind to make effective decisions regarding your physical health and finances. A power of attorney is a legal document that grants power to the person who's been chosen to act as your proxy when you're mentally unable to handle your own affairs.

General POA

When you want someone to have the ability to act comprehensively in your place—to pay your bills, talk to your bank, sign documents for you, and cancel credit card accounts—you will grant them general power of attorney.

Limited POA

A limited power of attorney is one who has a specific set of limits around what the proxy can and can't do in your name. For example, you might allow them to take care of just one document signing on a specific date when you are unable to make it.

Durable POA

A durable power of attorney, whether general or limited, is one that remains in effect should you become mentally incapacitated—such as being in a coma.

Power of Attorney for Healthcare

It's possible that the person you put in charge of your finances when you can't handle them is not the same person you'd put in charge of your medical decision-making when you're incapacitated. A power of attorney for healthcare allows you to name the specific individual you want to make those medical decisions.

Living Wills

A living will is a document that allows you to preselect certain healthcare decisions—such as whether you want the continued use of a respirator to prolong your life. When a medical decision isn't spelled out on a living will, or there is an additional complication or consideration, your power of attorney for healthcare may need to make the decision.

Day 28 Checklist

- ☐ Determine what kind(s) of power of attorney arrangements you want to have.
- ☐ Decide who you want acting as your POA.
- ☐ Visit Nolo.com or another site to download the forms and complete them.

Day 29

Your Senior Program Participation

You may not realize it, but there are many programs available to help seniors get discounts, gain political power, get financial assistance, increase their education, and more. Today, your goal is to look into the local and national programs that exist to help seniors in your area. Some programs and types to look into include:

- AARP: Seniors age fifty and over can join AARP to get discounts on travel and entertainment. Further, membership in AARP can help your voice be heard by local politicians.

- College programs: Many colleges allow senior citizens to attend their education programs and classes for free or at a heavy discount. In some cases, seniors may be able to attend as for-credit students while in other cases they may be restricted to auditing.

- Senior SNAP: Certain low-income seniors can benefit tremendously from the Senior Supplemental Nutrition Assistance Program (SNAP), which provides extra funds to help seniors afford healthy foods.

- Employment programs: Not every senior wants to stay out of the working world upon retirement. Some like to continue working, at least part-time. Others may find that retirement isn't as enjoyable as they thought it would be, so they want to go back to work full-time. But it can be hard to find work as a senior, which is why local and national senior employment programs that offer training and job matching, such as Senior Service America Inc., can help.

Millennials

In the decades before you retire, these senior programs will probably undergo many changes. Do new research as you get closer to retirement so you know what new programs are available for your retirement.

- Fitness programs: Seniors need specialized fitness routines and options that help ensure healthy, flexible bodies with better balance but that are low impact and easy to maintain. Programs such as Silver Sneakers and Active Choices can offer exactly what an aging body needs.
- Nutrition programs: Many seniors have trouble affording healthy foods on their fixed-income budget. Programs such as the Senior Farmers' Market Nutrition Program can help seniors get some extra money for spending on fresh fruits and vegetables at farmers' markets and roadside stands.

Baby Boomers

How many of these programs do you already qualify for? Find out and use them so you can immediately start to see the benefits—even if you aren't yet retired.

This list is by no means comprehensive. Stop by your local senior center or do a search online to get more ideas.

Day 29 Checklist

☐ Find out what senior programs are offered in your area.

☐ Consider contacting local churches and community centers to see if they have any special senior programs.

Day 30

Your Medicare

This is it—your final day of making your initial retirement plans! There isn't a lot to actually put into place today; you've handled most of that already. Today is all about research—but that doesn't mean you're getting off easy, because you're about to research one of the most complex benefits afforded to seniors and retirees: Medicare.

What Is Medicare?

Medicare is a federally established program that provides health insurance and benefits within the US to individuals who are sixty-five and older, as well as other special-needs people.

The benefits provided by Medicare are broken up into parts:

- Part A: Medicare Part A is hospital insurance, which covers any care you receive as an inpatient at a medical facility or nursing home.
- Part B: Part B covers regular medical expenses such as doctor bills and routine tests. Together with Part A, this is what's called Original Medicare.
- Part C: If you decide that you don't want Original Medicare, then you might instead choose Part C, which is a Medicare Advantage Plan (something I'll discuss in more detail later).
- Part D: Part D helps subsidize the expense of the prescription medication you need as a senior on Original Medicare. You will generally be expected to pay a deductible ($435 as of 2020) and then a co-insurance portion of 25 percent until you reach the out-of-pocket limit ($4,020 in 2020).

Understanding Medicare Advantage Plans

Instead of choosing coverage through Parts A, B, and D, you can choose a Medicare Advantage Plan. An Advantage Plan is more similar to the types of coverage you might have had while working—it's a policy issued by a health insurance company. It can be organized as an HMO or a PPO and can offer either network-restricted benefits or wider coverage options.

- HMO: A health maintenance organization (HMO) uses a network of providers that you are permitted to see, thus keeping coverage rates and copays low.

When you visit someone out of this network, you cover the full cost.

- PPO: A preferred provider organization (PPO) has a network of medical treatment providers but also provides some limited coverage when you visit out-of-network providers, even without a referral.

Advantage Plans can be helpful to seniors who need vision and dental coverage or coverage for care provided overseas. Their out-of-pocket spending caps and prescription drug coverage can make Advantage Plans a more affordable choice for some.

SAMPLE ADVANTAGE PLAN

⚠ This is only a summary. For detailed information about your plan, coverage and costs, please see the complete policy document.

Questions	Answers
What is the overall deductible?	**$500** PER PERSON **$1,000** PER FAMILY PREVENTIVE CARE EXCLUDED
Are there other deductibles for specific services?	**$300** PRESCRIPTION DRUGS DEDUCTIBLE
What is the out-of-pocket limit for this plan?	**$2,500** / PERSON **$5,000** / FAMILY IN-NETWORK ONLY
What is not included in the out-of-pocket limit?	PREMIUMS, SERVICES NOT COVERED BY THE PLAN, BALANCE-BILLED CHARGES
Is there an annual coverage limit for services provided?	NO
Is there a network of providers?	YES. SEE WEBSITE FOR LIST
What services are not covered by this plan?	SEE POLICY FOR COMPLETE LIST OF EXCLUDED SERVICES
Can I see a specialist without a referral?	YES

FIGURE 10

SAMPLE PLAN, NOT A GUARANTEE OF COVERAGE

FORM COURTESY OF CMS.GOV STANDARDIZED SUMMARY OF BENEFITS TEMPLATE

Medigap

If you choose Original Medicare (Parts A and B) over an Advantage Plan, you may choose to also get supplemental coverage through a Medigap, or Medicare Supplement, policy. These policies are issued by insurance companies and are designed to cover a portion of the copayments required with Original Medicare. Some policies also provide coverage for medical treatment received outside of the US.

OVERVIEW: MEDIGAP PLANS

Benefits	Medicare Supplement Insurance (Medigap) plans									
	A	B	C	D	F*	G	K	L	M	N
Medicare Part A coinsurance and hospital costs (up to an additional 365 days after Medicare benefits are used)	100%	100%	100%	100%	100%	100%	100%	100%	100%	100%
Medicare Part B coinsurance or copayment	100%	100%	100%	100%	100%	100%	50%	75%	100%	100%***
Blood (first 3 pints)	100%	100%	100%	100%	100%	100%	50%	75%	100%	100%
Part A hospice care coinsurance or copayment	100%	100%	100%	100%	100%	100%	50%	75%	100%	100%
Skilled nursing facility care coinsurance			100%	100%	100%	100%	50%	75%	100%	100%
Part A deductible		100%	100%	100%	100%	100%	50%	75%	50%	100%
Part B deductible			100%		100%					
Part B excess charges					100%	100%				
Foreign travel emergency (up to plan limits)			80%	80%	80%	80%			80%	80%
Out-of-pocket limit in 2019**							$5,560	$2,780		

* Plan F also offers a high-deductible plan in some states. With this option, you must pay for Medicare-covered costs (coinsurance, copayments, and deductibles) up to the deductible amount of $2,300 in 2019 before your policy pays anything. (Plans C and F won't be available to people who are newly eligible for Medicare on or after January 1, 2020. See previous page for more information.)

** For Plans K and L, after you meet your out-of-pocket yearly limit and your yearly Part B deductible ($185 in 2019), the Medigap plan pays 100% of covered services for the rest of the calendar year.

*** Plan N pays 100% of the Part B coinsurance, except for a copayment of up to $20 for some office visits and up to a $50 copayment for emergency room visits that don't result in an inpatient admission.

FIGURE 11

CHART COURTESY OF MEDICARE.GOV UNDER THE CREATIVE COMMONS PUBLIC DOMAIN DEDICATION

Important! Starting January 1, 2020, Medigap plans sold to people who are new to Medicare won't be allowed to cover the Part B deductible. Because of this, Plans C and F won't be available to people who are newly eligible for Medicare on or after January 1, 2020. If you already have either of these 2 plans (or the high deductible version of Plan F) or are covered by one of these plans before January 1, 2020, you'll be able to keep your plan. If you were eligible for Medicare before January 1, 2020, but not yet enrolled, you may be able to buy one of these plans.

Day 30 Checklist

☐ Start researching the various Medigap and Advantage Plan options and compare them to find the ideal option for you.

☐ Find out the date you need to sign up for Medicare to avoid penalties.

Glossary

Back-end load: A sales charge on the sale of a mutual fund.

Capital gains: The profit made on the sale of an asset, such as a stock or real estate. Gains are taxed either at long-term rates when they've been held for a year or more, or short-term rates when they've been owned for less than a year.

Compound interest: Interest paid to a principal sum that goes on to earn more interest.

Dollar-cost averaging: An investing strategy that involves the ongoing, regular purchase of a set amount of a certain asset in order to help drive down the average purchase price.

Durable power of attorney: A type of authority that remains in effect even after the grantor has become incapacitated.

Exchange traded funds (ETF): Similar to a mutual fund, an ETF is a bundle of securities chosen to help the fund perform similarly to a chosen exchange.

Fixed annuity: A contract issued by a life insurance company that guarantees the security of principal paid through a lump sum or periodic payments. Fixed annuities also guarantee a certain rate of interest.

Fixed indexed annuity: Similar to a fixed annuity, but with growth based on the performance of a chosen index.

Front-end load: A sales charge on the purchase of a mutual fund.

Guaranteed minimum withdrawal benefit: An additional rider added to certain annuity contracts that guarantees set lifetime payments.

Immediate annuity: An annuity contract in which a one-time payment is made and guaranteed income starts immediately.

Irrevocable life insurance trust: A trust that is made the owner and beneficiary of a life insurance policy. Irrevocable trusts cannot be changed once the grantor has gifted assets to the trust, unless the beneficiary permits the changes.

Mutual funds: Funds that invest in a variety of underlying assets such as bonds, stocks, and fixed investments.

Medicaid: A healthcare program funded by the government to help low-income families and individuals pay for medical expenses.

Medicare: A federally established program that provides health insurance and benefits within the US to individuals who are sixty-five and older, as well as other special-needs people.

Medicare parts:

- Part A: Medicare Part A is hospital insurance, which covers any care you receive as an inpatient at a medical facility or nursing home.
- Part B: Part B covers regular medical expenses, such as doctor bills and routine tests. Together with Part A, this is what's called Original Medicare.
- Part C: If you decide that you don't want Original Medicare, then you might instead choose Part C, which is a Medicare Advantage Plan.
- Part D: Part D helps subsidize the expense of the prescription medication you need as a senior on Original Medicare. You will generally be expected to pay a deductible ($435 as of 2020) and then a co-insurance portion of 25 percent until you reach the out-of-pocket limit ($4,020 in 2020).

Medicare Advantage Plan: A policy issued by a health insurance company that can be chosen instead of Original Medicare. It can be organized as an HMO or a PPO and can offer either network-restricted benefits or wider coverage options.

Medicare Supplement Plan: Policies issued by insurance companies that are designed to cover a portion of the copayments required with Original Medicare.

Power of attorney: Authority granted to another person so they may make financial, legal and/or medical decisions on your behalf.

Provisional income: The combination of gross income, tax-free interest, and 50 percent of Social Security income. This number can determine whether any portion of Social Security benefits will be taxable.

Revocable trust: A trust that allows the grantor to make changes even after gifting assets to the trust.

Required minimum distribution: A distribution that you are required to begin taking from a Traditional IRA every year starting in the year in which you turn 72.

Social Security break-even point: The date at which you start taking more out of Social Security than you paid into the system.

Stock market indexes: Collections of stocks, such as the Dow Jones Industrial Average and the S&P 500, that allow for the measurement and tracking of performance of the index's portion of the market.

Tax deferral: The ability to delay tax payments to a later date.

Term life insurance: An inexpensive policy designed to offer coverage for a limited period of time. Can often be converted to a whole life policy.

Universal life insurance: A type of permanent life policy with flexible premiums and options for cash value growth. When the cash value performance is tied to subaccounts modeled after stock indexes and has guarantees against losses, it is an index universal life insurance policy.

Variable annuity: Annuity contracts in which you choose subaccounts with a variety of stock and bond investments that are managed by professional money managers, much like mutual funds are.

Whole life insurance: A policy with a guaranteed, fixed premium and death benefit, which also accrues cash values and is designed to offer coverage for your entire life.

Acknowledgments

For a very long time, I've considered myself a frustrated writer. I can't tell you the number of times I've put pen to paper (yes—ink pen and real paper) and started a book, only to find myself too discouraged, distracted, or busy to keep writing.

This book—an actual finished book—was a long time coming, and I couldn't have done it without the contributions of a great many people.

To my clients, thank you for reminding me every day about what's important in life and for entrusting me with your finances and your futures. It is an honor to serve you.

To my fellow agents and advisors, thank you for always being open and sharing as new products, laws, and practices flood our industry.

To my beta readers—Cynthia, Steven, Kelly, Michael, and Diane—thank you for taking the time to read the early stages of this book and giving me your feedback and questions.

To my wife and kids, thank you for always being supportive.

Finally, to my editor, Yolander Prinzel, your insightful feedback and commentary helped me get this done. You are amazing!

Patrick T. Lyman, CAS, CSA, RFC, RHU

About the Author

Author Patrick T. Lyman has spent forty-six years in the financial industry. As president of Compass Financial Solutions, his mission is to assist individuals and business owners in achieving their retirement income goals with strategies that focus on safety and security. His commitment to his career and clients shows in his dedication, experience, certifications, and industry memberships.

Patrick is a member of the American Society of Financial Services Professionals and the International Association of Registered Financial Consultants. He first qualified for membership in The Million Dollar Roundtable in 2005. Membership in this exclusive, premier financial services industry group requires the ability to maintain high service standards focused on enhancing clients' lives, and a steadfast commitment to a strict code of ethics. In 2016 he became a Qualifying and Life member—an honor reserved for those who uphold the group's ethical standards and production requirements for ten or more consecutive years.

He is also a member of the American Society of Certified Senior Advisors and has been awarded their *certified senior advisor* designation after completing an extensive educational program focused exclusively on issues of financial importance to seniors.

For the last several years, Patrick has regularly conducted educational retirement planning workshops designed to help people determine how to achieve their retirement goals. His commitment to educating people about retirement planning reflects his passion for this issue.

Patrick believes that to be dedicated to his clients, he must also be committed to his community. His efforts to strengthen the financial independence and knowledge of community members is shown through his many educational workshops conducted at various YMCAs in the tri-county area, his involvement in the Rotary Club of Upper Darby/Lansdowne, the Delaware County Police and Firefighters Organization, and his membership in the Honorable Order of the Kentucky Colonels, a charitable and philanthropic institution founded in 1813.

Patrick currently resides in Drexel Hill, Delaware County. He is married with three children and four grandchildren. His oldest son is a member of the United States Army Special Forces and has served several tours in Afghanistan and Iraq. As a former president of the Upper Darby/Lansdowne Rotary Club and member in good standing since 2004, Patrick has a long history of activity in a variety of civic and volunteer groups within the community.